HISTORY OF THE
CHURCH IN NAMIBIA

Shekutaamba Nambala

Edited by Oliver K. Olson

ISBN 0-89579-303-2

Table of Contents

Editor's Introduction

THE TITLE OF this book is correct. It is about the church in Nambia—which is to say *all* the churches. Its author is Lutheran Pastor Shekutaamba V. Nambala, himself a Namibian. At the Lutheran Theological College at Mapumulo, South Africa, he wrote a diploma thesis on "Ovambo Culture and Rituals Before and After Penetration by Christian Worship."

The present volume is the first-ever history of the Namibian church and was written while Pastor Nambala studied at Luther Theological Seminary in St. Paul. It was published serially in *Lutheran Quarterly* in four installments: Autumn and Winter of 1987 and Summer and Autumn of 1988.

This paperback edition is a gift to Namibian students from the Lutheran Church Women of St. Paul's Church, Collingswood, New Jersey, from funds gathered after St. Paul's Pastor, Louis A. Smith, returned to the United States with praises for the "truly Christian country" he had learned to love. Pastor Smith, who taught at the Paulinum, a theological seminary for native seminarians from 1987 to 1989, claims to be the only teacher of theology ever forced to clear his classroom of goats. His historical classroom is in Otjinbingwe, eighty kilometers as West African crows fly, west of Windhoek.

The cover, "Windhoeck People Pray for Peace," and other illustrations are from the legacy of the late Namibian artist, John Ndvevasia Muafangejo (1943–1987). One, "Evangelical Lutheran Church Women's Meeting (Umhlangano, Wabasisikiasi)," depicting their sisters in faith, was chosen as a small thanks to the women of St. Paul's, Collingswood.

Oliver K. Olson
Editor, *Lutheran Quarterly*

Adam and Eve
John Muafangejo
1968 + 85
OVAMBO

Preface

THE DESERT THAT gives the land its name, the Namib, is the oldest in the world. Its dunes, running almost to the Atlantic's edge, are the highest. The few weltwitschia scattered across the desert only make the bareness more apparent. The mountains that dot the landscape from South to North are, for all their beauty, stark and harsh. Were it not for the Namib Desert in the West and the Kalahari in the East, surely the Khomas highlands in the center would deserve the name. The "rivers" spend most of their time without water. And coastal areas bear names like the "Skeleton Coast." Even use of the major natural resources, minerals, requires brute force. A quick tour of the natural environment leads one to agree with the native assessment that this is "The Land God Is Angry With."

Its political history might lead to the same conclusion. Warring tribes antedated the arrival of Europeans, and their arrival brought colonialism. Germans took Namibia, part of their spoils from the European Colonial Conference of 1884, and ruled it with an iron fist. They called it "South West Africa." The native population was reduced by force of arms to slavery, and resistance was met with a slaughter of genocidal proportions. One of the colonial administrators was the father of Herman Goering; another, Lothar von Trotha, called his policy "Vernichtung" (extermination), a term used later to describe National Socialist death camps.

When World War I "freed" the land from German control, it was only to create more space for South Africa, even then on the way to becoming a legally racist state. Namibia's pleas were ignored by the rest of the world; her fate was manipulated by the great powers. She gained her independence only after a twenty-two-year guerilla war. "The Land God Was Angry With," indeed.

And yet. Since this book is about the Church of Jesus Christ and her Gospel, there is always "and yet." It is hard to know exactly where to begin saying "and yet." Does it begin when the Nama people from the Cape Area of present-day South Africa crossed the Orange River and brought with it what they had learned of the Christian Faith from the Dutch? Does it begin with the arrival of missionaries from the London Missionary Society? In any case, God remembered Namibia and sent his Gospel. A church was founded that participated in—perhaps even fostered—a movement for independence, which. . . . But then, it is always hard to determine just what the full influence of consciences set free by the Gospel of Jesus. As Martin Luther said, the Christian life is hidden.

Shekutaamba Nambala has followed the story of God, the Father of Jesus Christ, remembering "The Land That God Was Angry With." His work, long overdue, is the first full-scale history of the Church in Namibia. It was a privilege for me to teach in that church, and it is a privilege to recommend it.

Louis Smith
Lent 1994

THE ANGEL CHASES SATAN IN 1979.

Namibia, A Country in Search of Self-determination

A T THIS CRITICAL TIME OF struggle, it becomes imperative for the Namibians to write their own history. This history has remained unwritten for many centuries. The little which is written has been the work of foreigners. The aim of this study is to attempt to collect basic data about the history of Namibia in which the Church, as the agent of God's Word of peace, forgiveness, justice, righteousness, and reconciliation, has been working for over 180 years. It is also the purpose of this study to build a foundation for future Namibian historians by recording most of the major dates, people, places and events. I do not claim that this study is the last word in scholarship; rather, it is a modest recording of events for future reference. However, when it is demanded, I do not hesitate to give interpretive analysis. I want to tell a story, but I want the story to be properly understood.

Namibia "is one of the most inaccessible regions of Africa"[1] and the "least known [because] its problems and complexities [are] the least understood."[2] Although the country is sparsely populated by less than two million people, it is the fifteenth largest country on the continent.[3] Namibia is one of the richest countries in Africa. Sadly, the majority of its inhabitants are ruthlessly exploited by foreigners with their huge, merciless mining companies and cattle ranches.[4]

Namibians today are oppressed and dehumanized, but they struggle to regain what is rightfully theirs. Namibia's capital city, /Ai-//Gams, is still decorated by the signs of European power and success from the time of colonial intrusion in which the Herero people were reduced from 80,000 to 20,000 and the Nama people from 20,000 to 9,700. The decimation of the population is a constant feature of European exploitation. Responsible people the world over are repelled by this long story of death.

From the first landing of the Portuguese on the west coast in 1484, Namibian history can be subdivided into different periods or stages: Pre-history to 1484; the period of explorers, traders and missionaries (1484–1884); colonialism under Germany (1884–1915); South African military administration (1915–20); Mandate and South African colonialism (1920–66); and South African illegal occupation and intensification of nationalism (1966 to present day, 1987). Although I am aware of these stages, I do not strictly follow them in my organization of this study.

Different names were used to refer to this great territory before it became known as Namibia in 1968. These former names refer either to the whole territory or parts of it, such as: Trans Gariep, Great Namaqualand (covers most of the southern parts), Damaraland (Hereroland—central parts), Ovamboland (covers some northern parts), or lately, German South West Africa or just South West Africa soon after South Africa seized the territory from the Germans in 1915. Today the majority of the people prefer that it be called Namibia as a unifying name against colonialism, tribalism, and ethnicism.

The population is comprised of ninety percent blacks. They are forced to live on ten percent of the land, while the less than ten percent of the population comprised of whites lives on ninety percent of the arable land under the oppressive rule of South Africa. The ten percent of the land on which the blacks live is further split into ten reserves (ghettos) for the purpose of ruling through division. Major indigenous language groups are: Damara-Nama, Herero, Kavango, Oshiwambo, Subia, San, and Tswana. Within these language groups there are many related languages and dialects. For example, Oshiwambo includes these languages: Oshindonga (Ndonga), Oshikwanyama, Otshikwambi, Otshingandjera, Oshimbalanhu, Oshikwaluudhi, Oshikolonkadhi and Shiunda (Eunda). Each of these Oshiwambo languages has its own different dialects. Further, there are German, Afrikaans, and English as "official" languages.

Education in Namibia is compulsory for whites but not for blacks. The highest education a black person is allowed to achieve is high school. There are no schools for blacks beyond high school in Namibia. Illiteracy is very high: more than sixty percent of the population. Nevertheless, there are capable Namibians ready to take charge of leadership in a free Namibia. Health services are very poor among the blacks. There is a high infant mortality rate (163 per 1,000) for blacks. Black children die mainly from malnutrition. The infant mortality rate among whites is 22 out of 1,000. While the amount of 214 rand per capita is spent on a black child's education, 1,500 rand are spent on a white child's education. On health services, 5.40 rand are spent on a black person, compared to 270 per capita on a white person. The income ratio of whites to blacks is 20:1, with the whites doing the minimum or easy jobs. Until recently, black women have been the most victimized in the salary ratio, receiving the lowest salaries of all.

Over eighty-five percent of Namibians are Christians, sixty percent of which are Lutherans. This means that over half of the Namibians today are Lutherans. Namibia received its first Lutheran missionaries from Germany (1842) and Finland (1870). Roman Catholic missionaries established themselves in 1896, although attempts had been made before that date. The Anglicans started missions in 1920 by serving English-speaking South African soldiers. Other denominations came in later. Membership in each denomination is related to the length of time the denomination has been in the country. Lutherans were the earliest to arrive; they are in the majority.

Namibia was a German colony when South Africa invaded the territory in late 1914 to defeat the Germans and occupy the land. In 1920 the League of Nations gave a mandate for Namibia to South Africa to administer the territory under a "C" mandate on behalf of Britain and as "a sacred trust of civilization." According to Article 22 of the League Covenant:

To those colonies and territories which as a consequence of the late war have ceased to be under the sovereignty of the States which formerly governed them, and which are inhabited by peoples not yet able to stand by themselves under the strenuous conditions of the modern world, there should be applied the principle that the well-being and development of such peoples form *a sacred trust of civilization,* and that securities for the performance of this trust should be embodied in this Covenant.

With the Second World War, the League of Nations gave way to the United Nations. All other former Mandate Territory was either independent or placed under the trusteeship of the United Nations. South Africa refused to place Namibia under the trusteeship. Namibia has been an explosive international issue in the United Nations since 1946. In 1966 the United Nations terminated South Africa's mandate over Namibia and the United Nations Council for Namibia was formed instead in 1967. The year of this revocation of the mandate status by the United Nations was also a year of historical decision for the Namibians' struggle for independence. Mr. Theo-Ben Gurirab, former SWAPO Permanent Representative to the United Nations and current SWAPO Secretary for Foreign Affairs, in his address on the occasion of the United Nations Fourteenth General Assembly Special Session on Namibia, reminded the international community with these words:

A few months prior to the termination of the mandate, the Namibian people themselves had taken an historic step forward in the war of national liberation. For one thing, we refused at that time, as we continue to do today, to be intimidated by the machinations and manoeuvres of the imperialists and their racist clients in Pretoria. How could we, who have been victims for so long of the most brutal and inhuman colonial legacy of genocide, concentration camps, forced labour, ruthless exploitation and unmitigated impoverishment by the marauding disciples and mercenaries of slave traders and dubious civilising and christianising missions, which have left in the wake of their activities, death, destruction and darkness, ever hope to get justice at the hands of the people whose hands are dripping with the blood of our people?[5]

From this quotation one can see that Namibians are getting tired of waiting for an independence that is purposely prolonged with unnecessary linkages and tactics. In the wake of South Africa's violation of International Law and its refusal to leave Namibia, the International Court of Justice in 1971 ruled that South Africa is illegally occupying Namibia. In 1973, on the international political front, the South West Africa People's Organization (SWAPO), which was organized in 1960 and has been waging guerrilla war since 1966, was recognized by the United Nations General Assembly "as the authentic representative of the Namibian people." SWAPO resorts to the use of armed struggle after many years of peaceful attempts and failures on the part of South Africa and other countries involved to listen to the pleas of the Namibian people. In 1978 the Security Council of the United Nations adopted Resolution 435 (R435-1978) calling for democratic election in Namibia under the supervision of the UNO. But South African and American administrations became reluctant and almost unwilling to allow the implementation of the resolution. They linked the presence of the Cubans in the sovereign state of the Republic of Angola with the Namibian case. Namibians categorically reject this linkage, seeing it as a well-calculated delaying tactic and as a way to maintain the illegal occupation of South Africa for the purpose of continuing to exploit and extract Namibian resources by the western countries against Decree No. 1 of the 1974 United Nations Council for Namibia for the Protection of the Natural Resources of Namibia, which says:

No person or entity, whether a body corporate or unincorporated, may search for, prospect for, explore for, take, extract, mine, process, refine, use, export, or distribute any natural resource, whether animal or mineral, situated or found to be situated within the territorial limits of Namibia. . . .

At present Namibia is one of the most militarized countries on earth with 100,000 South African troops stationed in the country at the ratio of one soldier per ten civilians to maintain and to insure that the colonial rule remains intact. The war is escalating daily and thousands of lives are lost on a daily basis. This war plus thousands of Namibians in exile pose a grave concern to the churches and history. This will become self-evident as we examine the details in the following chapters. With the experience of a history of displacements, Chief Hosea Kutako, one of the prominent chiefs and kings in the country, prayed forty years ago:

O God, you are the God of all the earth and the heavens. We are so insignificant. In us there are many defects. But you know all about us. For coming down from heaven you were despised and brutally treated by the people of those days. For those people you prayed because they did not understand what they were doing, and that you came only for what is right. Help us to struggle in that way for what is right. O Lord, help us who roam about. Help us who have been placed in Africa and have no dwelling place of our own. Give us back a dwelling place. O God, all power is yours in heaven and earth. Amen![6]

Namibia's history of colonialism and dispute has been felt within and without. Both internal and international communities for more than a hundred years have been preoccupied with its unsolved case. The Church is not exempted. International churches at large have been flooded with cries from the sister churches in Namibia calling for support in the struggle for justice, peace, decolonization, and reconciliation in Namibia before too much blood is shed. As a result, for example, the Thirteenth General Convention of the American Lutheran Church approved the following statement:

RESOLVED, that the American Lutheran Church designate November 2, 1986 (All Saints Sunday, the Sunday immediately following the 20th anniversary of the UN action on Namibia), as an occasion in ALC congregations for special concern and prayer for the freedom and self-determination of the Namibian people.[7]

This is just one of many international expressions of concern and involvement. The Catholic Institute for International Relations and the British Council of Churches put it this way:

The problem of the South African occupation of Namibia is essentially one of international law and international order, rightly in the hands of the United

Nations. But it is much more. Namibia shows in exaggerated form the deformities of a colonial economy, the ravages of the apartheid system given free rein for two decades, and the product of state violence, a population in revolt supporting a war of liberation whose interests are often the last to be considered. These are matters of grave concern for the world community for the Christian churches.[8]

The Church in Namibia is part and parcel of this history and many a time a victim of the prevailing vicious political system of apartheid and colonialism in the land given romantic names by the Europeans: "Land of Sand and Sun" and "The Land God Made in Anger."[9] In relation to the whole of Africa, J. J. Kritzinger in his research on the church in Namibia quotes Hans Jenny as saying: "Africa is a continent of extremes and contradictions; Southwest Africa is the representative example for the whole continent; climate, landscape and man make up the greatest conceivable contrasts."[10]

Nevertheless, Namibia as a country needs its own unique treatment which may not be found anywhere in Africa. This is the story to be told.

I

NAMIBIA IS LOCATED IN THE SOUTHWEST OF Africa as its former colonial name describes it: German South West Africa. It is bordered by Angola in the north, Zambia in the northeast, Botswana in the east, and South Africa in the south and southeast. The west coast is lined with the Namib sandy desert, fifty to seventy kilometers wide and stretching in length from the Orange River to the Kunene River. For many decades the Namib protected the Namibian interior from the Europeans' imperialistic penetration, until the nineteenth century when Europeans found a way in from both the north and the south. A description of the geography of Namibia is not complete without mentioning the Caprivi Strip (the Caprivi Concession, the Caprivi Zipfel—"Zipfel" in German means "tip" or "point"), which measures some 482 kilometers in length and between 30 and 105 kilometers in breadth. The Caprivi Strip is named after Georg Leo Graf von Caprivi di Caprara di Montecuccoli, a distinguished German soldier and Bismarck's successor as Imperial Chancellor between 1890 and 1894. Great Britain ceded the strip to Germany in 1893. The aim of the German government was to get an

NAMIBIA

access to the Zambezi River, to link Namibia to Tanzania (former German East Africa), and probably to prevent the Englishman Cecil Rhodes from penetrating northwards into the interior of Africa.

Namibia is described to be shaped like "a tall, top-heavy cooking pot with its handle."[11] Whatever the description, it is clear that Namibia is a vast territory covering an area of 824,295 square kilometers (317,827 square miles). It is larger than France and the United Kingdom combined and twice the size of California in the United States of America. It has an average distance of 1,200 kilometers from north to south and 800 kilometers from east to west. Most of the land consists of a high plateau with an average altitude of 1,080 meters above sea level.

The climate of Namibia is hot and dry with the annual temperature ranging from 16°C (60°F) on the west coast to 30°C (86°F) in the interior. The coldest temperature averages range from 4°C to 20°C (40°F–68°F). Namibia's climate is the driest in sub-Sahara Africa. Average annual rainfall is between fifty millimeters and five hundred millimeters (six to twenty-one inches). The territory's border rivers stem from countries having greater rainfall than Namibia. The Kunene, the Okavango and Kwando, the Zambezi and the Orange Rivers are perennial and all have flows which are significant relative to Namibia's water requirements. However, these are international rivers and other countries also have rights over these waters. International agreement would be needed, in particular, for three rivers, viz., the Okavango, the Kunene and the Orange.[12]

/Ai-//Gams (Otjomuise, Omukuto or Windhoek) is the capital city. Walvis Bay and Lüderitz are Namibia's two major ports, although South Africa claims the Walvis Bay enclave of 1,124 square meters as part of South Africa.

Namibia is rich in minerals, e.g., uranium, diamonds, copper, lead, zinc, tin, vanadium, silver, wolfram/tungsten, lithium ores, tantalite, salt, and potential oil. Namibia is also good for the raising of cattle, goats and karakul sheep, and the coast is full of fish and crabs. Maize, millet, nuts and other ground products are major agricultural products. Mining and agriculture are the major economic contributors. About ninety percent of Namibians spend part of their lives on the land.[13] Therefore, according to Namibia's Perspectives for National Reconstruction and Development,

A significant issue requiring attention after independence will be the need to contain the rural-urban migration which is certain to take place. . . . It is important that land policy is used as an instrument of achieving socio-economic transformation through the elimination of exploitative structures, both traditional and capitalistic.[14]

In most African countries there is more than one ethnic group. Namibia is no exception to this general phenomenon. Whenever the Namibians speak of national unity and independence today, there are those who are restricted by the love of separation, ready to discourage such aspirations on the basis of ethnic diversities. Ethnicity becomes a pretext for them to keep the Namibians apart, forgetting that most, if not all, countries the world over, including big united countries such as the United States of America, Russia and most European countries, are comprised of people of different ethnic groups. The background histories of those countries should not be ignored. As an example, we can take the history of southeastern Europe during the third century. Wallace-Hardill speaks of West German tribes or ethnics as follows:

The West Germans (those who in Tacitus' day occupied the Oder-Elbe region) were Franks, Alamans, Saxons, Frisians and Thuringians. The East Germans (distinct in dialect and customs from the West, and living east of the Oder) were Goths, Vandals, Burgundians, Gepids and Lombards.[15]

It is an historically unjustifiable argument in southern Africa to contend for and to enforce the diversity of ethnicism to the extreme for the sake of racial "purity." There is no country on the globe which can claim its people to be purely of one ethnic background. Ultimately, peace cannot be obtained on the basis of ethnic or racial lines of segregation. Diversities of ethnic backgrounds and cultures within a nation determined to shape its future are not to be reasons for schisms and enforced laws of segregations. A united nation is held together by a common spirit for freedom, self-determination and progress.

Therefore, with confidence we can examine the individual known origins and backgrounds of the Namibian people today. This is done not in the spirit of keeping them apart, but rather for the purpose of allowing them to appreciate themselves as part of the common struggle toward unity. Shivute U. Shivute, one of Namibia's emerging historians, puts it this way:

. . . People of different ethnic background . . . should not make *ethnicity* a big issue . . . to the cause of united struggle . . . it is through building an interdependent unit of such ethnic, cultural and linguistic variety that strong, rich and genuine national Namibian culture can be achieved.[16]

As we proceed in dealing with the Namibian peoples, it should be taken for granted that there was not a single tribe that did not believe in a Supreme Being. A sacred or holy fire as a symbol of blessings and prosperity was common to many tribes.

THE BASTERS (REHOBOTHERS)

The tribe which calls itself "Basters" or "Rehobothers" is not to be found in southern Africa before 1652 in the way we know them today. However, even before the arrival of white people in the region, intermarriage of different ethnic groups and races was possible and practiced. Unless we ignore the course of history, there is no single and pure race or ethnic group whatsoever. The formation of the Basters was a gradual process which took place over the course of many years. The Basters or Coloureds originated from the intermarriages of Europeans and slaves from Angola, Mozambique, Madagascar, Malaysia, Indonesia and other eastern countries. Secondly, they came from mixed blood of Europeans and the Khoikhoi and San (Bushmen) people. Thirdly, they came from the Khoikhoi and San people, as indigenous people of southern Africa and the slaves. These are the three sources which created the Basters.

The whites settled in the Cape Colony in 1652. Reports of intermarriage between whites and blacks goes back to 1657.[17] The story of Gert Kloete, a Dutch farmer in the Cape Colony is illustrative. His wife died sometime before 1750. Kloete then married a Nama (Khoikhoi) woman. They had a son, Jasper, who was disinherited by his brothers simply because he happened to be of "mixed" blood. When Jasper Gert Kloete married, he moved northward and resided in the surrounding area of Kamaggas. This family, together with other people of mixed blood, grew into a big community. By the 1830s, through the friendship between the London Mission Society missionary Heinrich Schmelen and the Kloete family, a Christian community was formed at Kamaggas. This community had its own rules, "which were finally codified under the Dutch title of Gemeenteordening, 'Community Organization,' and officially recognized by the Cape Town government in 1857."[18]

The Boer farmers of the Cape Colony and the growing number of white settlers in the area led the Cape government, by its Land Beacons Act, to remove the Basters from their beloved former place, Kamaggas, in 1865. As a result, the Basters, under the leadership of Johannes and Hermanus van Wyk, gathered their possessions and crossed the Orange River into Namibia in search of places to live in 1868. In Namibia, the Nama Chief Willem Swartbooi rented to them the Rehoboth district, where they settled in 1870. The arrangement however was apparently temporary, as the following suggests:

Hermanus van Wyk requested Willem Swartbooi to sell Rehoboth to the Basters. Chief Swarthooi replied that he did not intend to sell Rehoboth. But he wanted to *rent* it because he himself wanted to have it back later.[19]

In any event, Chief Abraham Swartbooi, in 1872, sold Rehoboth to the Basters. This transaction, not appreciated by the Nama tribe, led to future unrest between them and the Basters. But the Basters were determined to stay there. Thus Rehoboth became the Basters' republic governed under the *Vaderlike Wette* (Ancestral Law). Afrikaans, a language derived from Dutch, is the Basters' language. On the termination of German rule in Namibia in 1915, South Africa recognized Rehoboth as the Basters' "Fatherland" and today it is run as one of the ten "homelands" in Namibia.

Some people have attempted to distinguish between the Namibian Rehobothers (Basters) and the Coloured people of Cape Town, despite their similar backgrounds. According to Eschel Rhoodie:

The Coloureds have more or less the same racial background as the Basters but, unlike the Basters whose chief occupation is animal husbandry, the Coloureds are found mainly in the towns and cities where they are either employed or have their own business. Whereas the Basters have a chief and Counselors administering an area recognized as their exclusive homeland, the Coloureds have neither a distinct homeland nor a chief and Counselors.[20]

The South African whites regard the Basters and Coloureds as inferior to whites, but superior to blacks in general. For years most Basters have tended to affiliate themselves more with whites than with blacks. It does not require special intelligence to understand that in the light of the long-standing policy of racial segregation the Basters were put in a most difficult position. They belong to both parties. However, it is also natural to affiliate with the one regarded as "superior" or "powerful" until such time comes when polarization finally is brought to an end. The Commission of Inquiry regarding the Cape Coloured of 1938 came to this conclusion:

Though the Coloureds have always . . . tended to identify their interests as closely as possible with that of the Europeans', it is not possible to state exactly in general terms how large an infusion of European blood has taken place into the Cape Coloured. It is however an important constituent of their descent. Individuals range from those who obviously have little or no European blood to those who approximate so closely to pure European descent that they are able to "pass" as such, and there is often uncertainty and difficulty in distinguishing such "Coloured" from Europeans.[21]

Because of this background, a good number of Coloureds could escape into the white population without being noticed by those perpetuating the myth of racial purity.[22]

Names such as Beukes, van Wyk, Campbell, MacNab, Bezuidenhoudt and Diergaardt are very common among the Basters because the Basters' community can easily relate itself to different common ancestors. In the late nineteenth century the number of Basters was around three thousand and could be subdivided into four major groups:

1. Hermanus van Wyk, in Rehoboth itself
2. Klaas Swart, in Grootfontein (south)
3. Elias de Vries (Steinkop's), in Kalkfontein
4. David Vilander (Pella's People), in Rietfontein.[23]

Since most of the Europeans who came to settle in South Africa were Christians, they influenced some of their descendants as well. As a result, most of the Basters were Christians before they entered Namibia. In the Cape Colony, Rev. Peter Sterrenberg of the Rhenish Mission established a congregation among the Basters at De Tuin in 1864. Friedrich Heidmann became their pastor in 1866. When the Basters trekked to Namibia in 1870, Heidmann trekked with them. It was Heidmann who named the new place Rehoboth[24] after Genesis 26:22, "For now the Lord has made room for us, and we shall be fruitful in the land," as a remembrance of the Basters' displacement and removal by the Boers of the Cape Colony from the Cape.

It was not until very late, as it has been everywhere else in the country, that the missionaries were ready to hand over clerical power to the Rehobothers. In the Rehoboth district, Goagoseb became a pastor to the Damara congregation in 1949. Jakobus Beukes was pastor to the Basters congregation in 1953, and Apollos Xamseb became pastor to the Nama congregation in 1954.[25] Dr. Lukas Johannes de Vries, the first indigenous President of the Evangelical Lutheran Church in South West Africa (1972–79) and second President of Lutheran Churches Federation in Namibia, the United Evangelical Lutheran Church in South West Africa (UELCSWA) (1975–78), was of the Rehobothers by background.

THE CAPRIVIANS

Detailed material about the Caprivians was not available for this investigation. However, the following can be said. The Caprivians belong to the Bantu group of Africa, found today in Caprivi—a strip of land in the northeast of Namibia. In 1914 British troops invaded the Caprivi and it was placed under the control of the British protectorate of Botswana until it was entrusted to South Africa by the League of Nations in 1920 with the rest of Namibia as the League of Nations' mandate territory. Although South Africa subsequently delegated Caprivi's administration to the British High Commission in Botswanaland, it was taken back by the Namibian (South West Africa) administration in 1929. The Department of Bantu Affairs of South Africa has been directly administering Eastern Caprivi since 1939 with Katima Mulilo as its headquarters,

The people living in the Caprivi (west and east, as it is divided into two parts) today include the Mbukushu, Mafue, Mayeyi, Matotela, Mashi and Masubia. Outside Namibia the Caprivians are ethnically related to the Lozi (Luyana) and the Makololo (Bafokeng) people in the Barotseland of Zambia. The Lozi pastured great herds of cattle and practiced agriculture. The Makololo people are part of the Sotho people, who were driven off their ancestral lands in the Transvaal by Chieftainess Mantatisi (mother of Sikonyela) of the Batlokowa in about 1823. Thereupon , Sebetwane, the Makololo leader, led his people northwards. By 1840 the Makololo settled on the upper Zambezi after having subjected the Lozi people to their rule, which lasted for some twenty years.[26] Besides the vernaculars, most Caprivians spoke the Silozi language.

The family structure is various in that some of them are patrillineal while there are strong matrilineal characteristics among the Mafue.

In 1921 the Seventh Day Adventist (SDA) missionaries started working in East Caprivi. The Roman Catholic Church joined the SDA in the 1940s. The Dutch Reformed also followed in the 1960s, while the Lutherans are now in the process of considering a congregation there.

THE DAMARA

The Damara are people who were also called *Die Bergdamara* (or Mountain Damara) by the colonialists. They are so called because with the expansion of colonial power in Namibia, as danger threatened, the Damara retreated and settled themselves among the mountains which could not easily be raided by their enemies. *Van Sending tot Kerk* gives this explanation:

They are generally called Mountain Damara due to the following reasons. In the olden days the Damara lived by the Nama as their servants. When the Nama people were impoverished by the coming of the Europeans into South—and South West Africa, the Damara separated themselves from the Nama. The Damara settled among the difficult to penetrate mountains of South West. Therefore they were given the name "Mountain Damara" which is no longer popular today.[27]

The origin of the Damara is obscure, although they probably came into Namibia from the east. They are also ethnographically difficult to classify. In color and physical shape the Damara look like the Bantu people. In habits of life and language they are allied to the Nama and Ju (San) people. While their ceremonies bear some Nama and Bantu characteristics, some authors contend that the Damara

. . . are a group of true Negroes long isolated from others of their stock. They speak Nama but also use expressions which are not Nama and which, one theory goes, are derived from languages in the Sudan. Their ceremonies show both Nama and Bantu influences. They are skilful copper and iron smelters, and this art they are said to have learned from the Ovambo. One exotic theory maintains that the Nama are descendants of the ancient Phoenicians and the "Damara," that they inherited from the latter their language and from the former their colour.[28]

Although some scholars maintain that the Damara were originally a negro or Bantu tribe "who by an eddy in the tide of Bantu migration had been left stranded on the western shore of the Kalahari Desert,"[29] where they probably came into contact with the powerful Nama people, there is a need for more research to be done. This is necessary because some, like Rhoodie, are saying that the Damara "are not part of the great Bantu family of Central and Southern Africa, although they show Bantu influences,[30] while others are saying that "racially they are more like peoples of Central and West Africa."[31]

At the advent of the Europeans in Namibia, many of the Damara people were serfs of the Herero and Nama. It is not clear how they came to be servants of these people. They might have been suppressed and enslaved or perhaps they were hired by the Herero and Nama because of their arts of pottery and forging iron. There is a contradiction in sources as to whether the Damara received the arts of forging iron from the Ovambo or taught the arts to the Ovambo. It is also possible that the Damara became serfs in a different way.

The small groups of settlers [Damara] who arrived in Damaraland [Hereroland] were often split by accidental circumstances. Some men took local wives and stayed with the tribe of their in-laws while the other Dama trekked further.[32]

The Damara lived in Damaraland, which covers the same area as Hereroland. These are some of the indications that the two ethnic groups lived closely together in the pre-German colonialism and before the contemporary imposed system of South African "homelands." Damaraland covered north central Namibia near Otjiwarongo, and from the Kalahari in the east to the Namib Desert on the west coast. The Damara lived in closely related clans and kept some cattle and goats. Whether they had a king or chief depends on the term they used, "Gao-aob" (king) or "Dana khoib" (chief), with several advisers. The chief was both the political and ritual or spiritual leader simultaneously. He or she was understood to be the keeper of the ever-burning holy fire—the traditional symbol of prosperity, well-being and all good wishes. Some of the known leaders are: Saub, Narirab, Gariseb and his two sons Tsowaseb and Xhei Craub. Crawaweb, the son of Tsowaseb, was the fourteenth chief of the Damara. The Goreseb royal family is the most recent. Chief Cornelius Goreseb, who died in 1910, is from this family. Goreseb was given "protection" by the Germans from the Herero neighbors and granted the reserve around Okombahe, in which he, in return, had to provide laborers to the German government in the country. Before Chief Goreseb died, he foresaw the danger facing his people and prophesied, "I know that when I am no more, my people will be scattered like chaff in the wind."[33] Although the Namibians did experience several displacements even before his death, this prophesy became more true in the 1960s when thousands of Namibians had to flee their country because of political harassments and persecutions, something which continues to be a reality to this date.

If the Damara became serfs of the Nama through defeat, then it is probable that it was during the reign of Chief Tsowaseb that the

Nama defeated the Damara, made them their subjects and forced them to speak the Nama language. They were under severe punishment of death if one Damara was found speaking Damara.[34] In this way the Damara might have lost their language until today. Today the Damara speak Nama, a language with four clicks, namely: (/); (//); (!) and (≠). In order to distinguish the sounds of these clicks, one needs to know and be acquainted with the acoustic, auditory and articulatory phonetics as well as the places and manners of articulation.

The Damara believe in the Supreme Being (Xgamab), who is responsible for creation, rain and annual plant renewal. Erkki Laurmaa in his *Afrika j Uuningininomutenja* speaks about the Damara belief this way:

> They also know the Big One—"Nkeama" (God), who live in heaven. God is worshipped by singing and dancing. God restore and keep all goodness in heaven for his or her Damara people. Anyone who departs from this world will go along a broad way in which the ancestral spirits will meet him or her and lead him or her home to the city of Nkeama.[35]

They believe in life after death. For them death and sickness can be caused by God (Xgamab) or by the spirits of the dead. When death occurs, those still alive will burn down or abandon the hut of the deceased—of course, it was not of great value. It was also for health reasons, since the cause of death was not always known. In this way they could prevent more death in case of contagious diseases. For the Damara, as is common among the African people, "belief in providing for the needs of the dead seems to have been the root of the widespread custom of burying the body or burning victuals, utensils, treasure, slaves or wives."[36] This custom seems ridiculous to outsiders, but it is rooted in the strong belief that death is not the end of life. Therefore, life here on earth and life in the country of the dead are believed to bear some similar characteristics in terms of the possession of property and the need for the company of other people, especially those one happened to know.

There are several accounts among the Damara which parallel theologically some Christian doctrines. The one closest to the story of Jesus is the following. It is said to have happened during the reign of Crawaweb, the son of Tsowaseb, when

> . . . a great diviner appeared whose name was Qauseb, whose work was the interpretation of God's word. God (Xgamab) appeared in the shape of a huge eagle whose approach was accompanied by thunder and lightning. The eagle

then perched on a tree and began to speak human language so that all the people could hear him. Through this great bird, Qauseb knew everything that happened anywhere on earth. But it did not help him against death. One day during a battle against the Herero he was wounded in the knee and died on the battle-field. It is said that the eagle flew away with his soul. God never appeared again in this shape.[37]

Like other Namibian people, there are several tribes or clans within the Damara, such as the /Gowanin, !Koe≠gan, /Kai-o-daman, //Huruben, Namidaman, Tsoaxaudaman and the Dauredaman. The first people the Rhenish missionaries encountered in Namibia were the Nama, Herero and Damara successively. In 1871 the Rhenish Missionary Society established a mission station at Okombahe, the Damara headquarters. Today many Damara people are Christians. Eliakam //Hoebeb was the first black pastor at Okombahe in 1952.

THE HERERO (OVAHERERO)

The Herero are mainly found today in central and northwest Namibia. They are also in Angola and Botswana. The Herero include three tribes: the Ovaherero,[38] Mbanderu and Ovahimba (Ovatjimba). Sometimes Ovahimba and Ovatjimba are seen as two different tribes. The Herero speak Otjiherero, which, together with Oshiwambo (in Ovamboland) and Oshikavango (in Kavango), is known as a western Bantu language derived from what is known as the western dialects of Proto-Bantu (PB-A). Proto-Bantu (PB-X) proper "was spoken in a nuclear area around the Katanga about 200 A.D."[39]

According to the Herero legends and traditions, they were believed to have once lived in the far land of numerous lakes. Some authorities held that the Herero probably lived in Central Africa, where they migrated southward with other Bantu people. The Herero branched off and moved westward, arriving in Namibia by the sixteenth century. As to how they came to Namibia, there are two accounts. The first account says that they came from the north through Kaokoveld, where some of them settled, namely the Ovahimba, while others continued to the south during the seventeenth century. According to Rhoodie:

The third great influx of Bantu[40] was that of the Hereros, who crossed the Kunene River . . . from the Mossamedes Province of Angola. Part of the Herero nation remained behind in the Kaokoveld. . . . The main stream of the nation continued southward . . . until they . . . reached the Nama settlements. They were mistakenly called Damaras (black-skinned people) by the early White men from the Nama word for them and the country they occupied—from the Kaokoveld to Bechuanaland and south past Windhoek—became known as Damaraland. . . .[41]

The second account asserts that they came to Namibia from the northeast through Botswana. The Mbanderu remained behind in Botswana while the rest of the nation continued westward into the interior of Namibia. Some remained in central Namibia and others trekked to the Kaokoveld, from which some went beyond the Kunene River into Angola.[42]

Erkki Laurmaa gives this further description of the Herero migration:

. . . the Herero ancestors lived at big lakes in the heart of Africa. They migrated with other Bantu people. They settled in Botswana. As they moved from the springs of the Niles, they continued their contact with the people of Egypt and other people of northern regions for hundred of years. When they came into Botswana, the Herero formed two nations. One of these two nations was not at peace with the people of Botswana. As a result this one nation was expelled from Botswana (ca. 1550) and went to settle in Kaokoveld (Kaokoland). They had a lot of herds. To get pasture and water for their animals, most of these Herero left the Kaoko and came down as far as Omaruru and Swakopmund (ca. 1650).

When the rain seasons were good, some of them went back to Kaokoland to keep their animals safe from attack by other nations. Some of those who remained in Kaokoland became poor and were named "Ovahimba." Those who remained in Botswana looked after their herds along the Lake Ngami. Eventually the two Herero nations formed contacts until those who were in Botswana moved to Namibia. They are called Ovambanderu. They settled at Epukiro and Gobabis.[43]

As to the time of the arrival of the Herero in Namibia, I agree with Gray that "1550, the date generally given for their arrival, may well be too late."[44]

The Herero are known for their wealth in cattle, sheep and goats. Wellington describes them as people of a Hamitic-Negro mixture background and "owing to their conservative habits and their tendency to racial exclusiveness, they have preserved many distinctive physical and social traits."[45] The racial exclusiveness of any ethnic group in Namibia is challenged today by many nationalists, including Ovaherero, who see racial segregation and exclusiveness as a disaster, contributing to the disunity of the Namibian people.

The Herero family system is both patrilineal (oruzo) and matrilineal (eanda), which is unusual. Ties of affection between parents and children are very strong. Barrenness is regarded as a misfortune. The elders and leaders are deeply respected. Traditionally, when sickness occurs, according to Sir James George:

A sick person is carried round and round the sacred fire. A pot is cooking on it, containing meat killed for the purpose. His friends, as they carry him round the fire sing a prayer: "See, Father, we have come here with this sick man to you, that he may soon recover."[46]

The Herero believe in Mukuru (or Ndjambi), who is omnipresent and everlasting. Mukuru is at peace with all people. Mukuru is trustworthy and does not need anything. People do not need to give Mukuru anything. However, the Herero venerate their ancestors with the idea that the ancestors will pray to Mukuru on their behalf in times of need. This practice conveyed the belief in life after death even before Christianity spread among the Herero. When death occurred, the Herero slaughtered the dead person's goats and ate them, believing that the spirits of the goats would go to the owner's spirit, wherever it was, and that it would need them.

The history of the Herero was not always peaceful. Although there were tribal conflicts over cattle and grazing areas, their contact with European rule brought them much suffering. This happened especially through the German "infamous genocide campaigns of 1904–7" under the leadership of "a German specialist in human extermination,"[47] General von Trotha. It is estimated that of 80,000 only 20,000 Herero remain alive. However, according to Kerina, when the Germans ordered the Herero "half dead from hunger and thirst" to surrender, they obeyed and the refugees who asked for help were placed in concentration camps. In July 1906 the number of Herero was counted—17,000 left of a total population of 97,000.[48] Kerina describes the Von Trotha genocide further:

This was not a war, but an indiscriminate massacre by bayoneting, burning, hanging and poisoning of young and old. Within a year, out of a population of 97,000 Hereros, there remained 20,000 starving fugitives and of 130,000 Namas and Damaras only 37,743 remained. German losses were 179 officers and 2,169 men killed.[49]

The genocidal tradition of the Germans was further experienced by the Jews, who in the Second World War lost over six million people under Adolf Hitler's Nazi regime. It is not surprising to learn that during World War II the German population in Namibia were strong supporters of the Nazi party.[50]

The Christian mission among the Herero was founded in 1844, when the Rev. Carl Hugo Hahn established a mission station at Otji-kango (Neu-Barmen). However, mission work flourished only after the subjugation of the Herero in the holocaust of 1907.

One Chronology of the Herero Chiefs

Name	Years of Reign	Place of Burial
Kengeza	ca. 1500s	Kaokoveld
Batje and/or his uncle Kaundja	ca. 1550	Kaokoveld?
Mbingana	ca. 1580	Kaokoveld
Kasupi	ca. 1610	Kaokoveld
Tjoutuku	ca. 1640	Kaokoveld
Tjituka	ca. 1670	Kaokoveld
Mbunga	ca. 1700	Kaokoveld
Mutjise	ca. 1740–70	Okahandja?
Tjirue	ca. 1770–1800	Okahandja
Tjamuaha	ca. 1800?–1861	Okahandja
Maharero kaTjamuaha	1861–90	Okahandja
Samuel Maharero (son of Maharero)	1890–1904	Ukahandja
	1904–23 exiled	
Fredrik Samuel Maharero	exiled with his father in 1904 to Botswana	(+ 1952)
Hosea Kutako	1904–70	Okahandja
Clemens Kapuuo	1970–78	Okahandja
Kuaiima Riruako	1978–	

Other Chiefs

Zacharias and/or Willem Zeraua of Otjimbingwe (ca. 1907)
Kahitjene of Okahandja and contemporary to Tjamuaha and then to
    Maharero
Tjetjo, contemporary to Samule Maharero
Katuneko, contemporary to Tjamuaha
Abraham Kukuri of Otjozasu

Solomon Aponda of the Mbanderu of Barmen (ca. 1870s)
Kandjizei and the father of Chief Ndjiharine of Omburo (ca. 1830s)
Oseu, the father of Chief Kandjii of around Okahandja/Windhoek
Tjiraura
Katjihuiko of the Mbanderu

THE KAVANGO (OVAKAVANGO)

A Swedish trader, Charles John Andersson, in search of the route
to the Kunene River via Omandombe in order to avoid passing
through the Ovambo land, reached intead the Okavango River in
1857. Earlier, in July 1852, Andersson reached Lake Ngami. The
Okavango River was "discovered" after returning from his visit to
Sweden and England. Along the banks of the river, on both sides,
lived the five Okavango tribes. These include the Kwangari, Bunja,
Sambiu, Gciriku and Mbukushu as part of the western Caprivi nation. The Kavango are historically an offshoot of the Ovambo people. Gerhard Tötemeyer contends that "it can be assumed that the
Kavangos and the Ovambos, coming as a joint group from the east,
first migrated southwards and thereafter westwards past the headwa-
ters of the Zambezi, to the bank of the Okavango River."[51]
Whenever we are dealing with African tribes and nations, we
should always keep in mind that the partition of Africa by the Europeans was done without any consideration of the African people. Roland Oliver and Anthony Atmore put it this way: "European powers
partitioned Africa among themselves with such haste, like players in
a rough game, that the process has been called 'the scramble for Africa'."[52] It was so rough that they did not care what happened to the
Africans as long as they got a share of lands and control. This process
took two stages: the partition "on paper" of about 1879–91 and the
partition "on ground" in about 1891–1901. Although Germany was
almost late in the scramble, it managed to get a fair share as a result of
the Berlin Conference of 1884–85.
The Kavango settlement on both sides of the river resulted in the
Kwangari and Mbukushu languages being spoken on both sides.
The partition of Africa by the Europeans divided the Kavango people, so that some were taken under Portuguese control and others became subjects of the German colonialists in Namibia. Today, under
the establishment of the South African "homeland" system—which
divides the country into separate "homelands" for different ethnic

groups—Okavangoland on the Namibian side has become one of the ten "homelands."

The balkanization of Namibia cannot easily be bypassed without comment. The arbitrary division of Namibia into "homelands" (bantustans) by South Africa is a denial of national identity, ignoring the common historical roots of the indigenous people of Namibia. The Okavango "homeland" is one of the sources of cheap black labor to the white minority today.

The Okavango people believe and worship Karunga, praying in their annual Nyambinyambi ceremony that he provide rain and all other needs. It was not until the Roman Catholic church established a mission station at Nyangana in 1910, and in 1913 at Andara, that the Church was introduced there for the first time. The Finnish Mission Society established its mission contacts in Kavango in 1926 through the travels of the Rev. Emil Närhi. Their first mission station was founded at Nkurenkuru in 1929.

THE NAMA[53]

The Nama history is perhaps the most interesting of any people in Namibia. The Nama ethnic group produced the courageous leaders in Namibian history of the eighteenth and nineteenth centuries. In the mid-nineteenth century, the Nama people could be found almost throughout Namibia, from Sesfontein in the northwest to the Orange River banks in the south. No other group of people in the Namibia of that time could claim a wider access to the country than the Nama and San people. The San could be found in parts of southern Angola, Namibia, Botswana and South Africa.

The Nama people include those of Khoikhoin (Hottentot) and Orlams backgrounds. Jan Knappert defines the term "Hottentot" as follows:

Hottentot is the generic name for all the peoples who now live exclusively south of the Zambesi, mostly in Namibia and South Africa and who belong to a particular race speaking a closely related group of languages unrelated to any other language in Africa. . . . The origin of the word (Hottentot) is unknown apart from its being the Dutch word for these peoples. . . . The Hottentots are divided into the following subgroups: the South Africa Hottentots, consisting of . . . the Griqua . . . the Kora-na, and the Cape Hottentots who are now all Afrikaans-speaking. In Namibia there are three further groups, the Saan, the Nama and Dama . . . Oorlams. . . .[54]

By the mid-1800s the Nama people included these tribes from the north to the south of Namibia:

1. Ounin or !Gome = Topnaars, "Points People" in Sesfontein, Kaokoveld, led by Caichab and in Walvis Bay and Rooibank led by the Heibib family

2. //Khou-/gŏan = Swartboois, "Little Defenders" or "//Khou's Children" in Franzfontein

3. //Ai-Xa-//Ain = Afrikanders (Afrikaners), "Warrior People" in /Ai-//Gama (Windhoek) and on the banks of the Orange River, led by the family of Afrikaner

4. Gei-/Khauan - Amraal, "Numerous Division" in Gobabis led by the Lambert family

5. !Kowesin - Witboois, "Suppliants" in Gibeon led by the Witbooi family

6. //Khouben = Rooi Nasie (Red Nation), "Great Defenders" in Hoachanas led by Cornelius Oasib

7. /Hei-/Khauan or !Konan = "Buff Division" or Goliath's Volk with their center in Berseba

8. !Aman led by the Booi family in Bethanie

9. !Kara-gei-khoin - Franzmanns, "Various Big People", led by the Koper family with their center in Gochas

10. //Hawoben = Veldschoendraers, "Sandalwearers", of Quanib and led by the Ses family

11. !Karo-!ŏan - Tseib led by Jonathan Tseib around Keetmanshoop

12. !Gam-nun = Bondelswarts, "Black Bundles", in Warmbad led by the family of Christian Bondelswarts

13. //O-Gein = Groot Doden, who were under the leadership of the Aimab //Gein family on the upper Fish River.[55]

Ruth First gives the two general groups of the Nama people as follows:

The Nama clans are generally grouped into two sections: those who settled in the country after their migration southwards long before the arrival of the other tribes and the Orlams peoples, who passed through the country on their way into South Africa, lived south of the Orange River for a while, and then returned, before the pressure of White settlement, speaking Cape Dutch and using horses and rifles, in the eighteenth and nineteenth centuries.[56]

The !Kowesin, !Konan, !Aman, //Ai-Xa-//Ain and Gei-/Khauan belong to the Orlams group. *Orlam* is derived from a Malay word which means "foreigner."[57] It was from this group that great leaders and war commanders of that time were produced, such as Afrikaner and his brother Titus and Jager and Jonker Afrikaner, the two sons of Afrikaner. At times these men used their military powers too excessively and ruthlessly, plundering and showing their power over the little and powerless tribes from the Orange River up to Windhoek. Chief Hendrik Witbooi "the Great" (ca. 1825–1905) was one of the impressive Namibian leaders from this group. Witbooi was everything from progressive statesman, advocator for national unity, first guerrilla leader to church elder, "evangelist" and accomplished diarist. He is regarded today as a national hero. The rest of the group belonged to the so-called Nama "proper" who stayed behind in Namibia when the Orlams went further to the south.

The Orlams group migrated back to Namibia from the Cape about 1770. Some of them might have come along with the Basters group in 1868, in which case some were already Christians through the London Mission Society, the Wesleyan Methodists and the Rhenish Society missionaries in Little Namaqualand (south of the Orange River).

The Nama fat-tailed sheep are associated with those of Syria and Lebanon. They also had the best cattle and goats. According to Erkki Laurmaa, the Nama had their own arts of doing things, as can be seen from the following quotation:

The Nama did not live in booths like the San. They built for themselves moveable houses which they took along whenever they moved. They had also small gardens for beans and tobacco. Maybe due to their much movements, the Nama could not keep regular large fields for growing crops. . . . They are brave, clever and artistic. . . .[58]

One of the earliest accounts on the Nama was that of the Rev. Barnabas Shaw of the English Wesleyan Methodist Missionary Society, who with his friend Archbell left Lily Fountain, on the Khamies Berg in Little Namaqualand, to go northward across the Orange River on March 25, 1820. They crossed the Orange and arrived in Namibia (Great Namaqualand) on April 27, 1820. After fourteen weeks in Namibia Rev. Shaw returned to Khamies Berg and transmitted to the mission committee his account of the Nama of Namibia. Because the account is so classic, no apology for its length and insertion in this study is required, despite some disagreements we might have about its contents. Though it focuses upon the Nama people it also serves to describe in many ways other peoples of Namibia.

The Great Namaquas are, doubtless, of the same origin with the bushmen on the borders of the colony, and of the Little Namaquas within its boundary. They differ much from the Caffres and Bechuanas on the east, as also from their nearest neighbors, the Damaras on the west.

The figure of the Namaquas is by no means without attraction. They are generally taller than the Hottentots within the Colony, and are erect and well-proportioned. Their color is of a yellowish brown, though this is only apparent from their hands and faces, the rest of their bodies being discolored by grease and dirt.

Their disposition is mild and fearful, and, towards those who treat them with humanity, they are perfectly harmless. Honesty is portrayed in their countenance, and they are by no means void of affection for their families and connections. They will share the last morsel in their possession with one who is hungry, and reflections are cast upon any, who, to use their own expressions, "eat, drink or smoke alone". We not only travelled amongst them in perfect safety, but they liberally supplied all our wants, and were ready to render us every possible assistance. During the time that the Dutch had possession of the Colony, plundering parties were frequently sent out amongst these tribes, who not only took away their cattle, but committed the greatest barbarities. The Namaquas, as might be expected, sought revenge, and some of the plunderers met with the fate they justly deserved, whilst others were constrained to flee for their lives. Notwithstanding the cruelties, however, which they have experienced from Christian savages, missionaries may travel amongst them without danger.

Their huts, like those of the Little Namaquas, are perfect hemispheres, formed of the boughs of trees, and covered with matting; but the sedges of which their mats are made being of inferior kind, their hovels have but a mean appearance. Some of them may properly be called rich, as they possess immense numbers of horned cattle, besides goats and sheep.

We were frequently surprised at the return of their cows and oxen from the fields: clouds of dust, seen floating in the air on every side of the village, were continuing to approach each other, till the cattle which raised them were all brought together into one fold, where they remained for the night. They delight much in their cattle, and, like the Caffres, they turn the horns of their favorite ones in every direction which fancy to them as ornamental.

Their chief subsistence is animal food and milk: they have no bread nor vegetables, but there are roots that grow spontaneously in the field, which they gather and eat. They likewise use a sort of grass-seed, much resembling our English rye-grass, but of a heavier body. This, after being cleaned, is mixed with milk, and makes a good substitute for oatmeal. They do not, however, gather it themselves, but steal it from the nests of the laborious ants. The milk is sometimes drunk sweet as taken from the cows, but it is more generally put into vessels to coagulate, in which state it is supposed to be more nutritious.

Their dress is similar to that of the surrounding tribes. Many of the males wear a belt about the waist, to which is hung in front a case made of jackal's skin: others have a covering of soft leather, and the more wealthy have, in addition, a sort of wheel suspended at the end of an ornamented girdle. The wheel is formed of thick leather, and set with beads of copper or iron. Their krosses or cloaks are composed of the skins of sheep, jackals or wild cats, and also serve for their nightly covering. Sandals are almost in general use; and are either made of a bullock's hide, or the prepared skins of wild animals. The females wear a little apron, ten or twelve inches in breadth, and as many in length, formed of skin, and ornamented with various tassels, reaching to the knee. Some of them make caps of skin for their heads, and others cover them with the cured maws of sheep or calves.

They have ornaments of ivory, copper and iron rings on their legs and arms, and are much attached to beads, with which their wrists and necks, and sometimes their waists, are decorated. A red powder mingled with fat, and profusely laid on the head, forms, in their estimate, a rich pomatum. The females use various sorts of paint, with which they daub their cheeks. And here their difference of taste is displayed; some using red, others brown, and some a jet black, being a composition of charcoal and fat blended together.

Each tribe or clan is governed by a chief, who attends to the forms handed down from generation to generation. The chief receives the hinder part of every bullock which is slaughtered; this he distributes amongst the males of his village, all of whom are called his soldiers. He also collects a sufficiency of milk by the door of his hut, to deal out amongst the poor and the needy. On the death of his wife, every male who has arrived at years of maturity, gives him a cow, which, after a certain number of years, is again returned. A part of every animal taken in hunting is required by the chief, and though it should be in a state of putrefaction before it can be brought to him, he nevertheless demands his right.

The Great Namaquas carry with them their ancient weapons, the bow and arrows. The latter are preserved in a case or quiver, and are deeply poisoned. The assagay, which is a sort of spear fixed to the end of a tapering shaft, is in general use; in throwing this weapon they are remarkably expert; but they are alarmed at fire-arms, and will, if possible, make their escape from them.

Their petty wars generally originate respecting their cattle, but they are seldom of a serious nature. Their engagements may generally be compared to the sham-fights of children; yet, if Bushmen or others have stolen their cattle, a commando is dispatched to retake them, in doing which, death is sometimes the consequence.

In many things they are exceedingly superstitious, and their sorcerers exercise various tricks amongst them, to which most of them give credence. When a person is sick, the sorcerer is sent for, who examines the place where the pain is seated, and privately letting a small bit of wood fall upon it, he declares it has come out of the sick man's flesh. Sometimes he cuts off the first joint of the little finger of his patient, pretending that the sickness will go out with the blood: of this we had numerous proofs, in persons whom we saw, who had lost the first, and some the second joint of the little fingers. On such occasions, the sorcerer demands the fattest sheep in the flock, which is killed and feasted upon. Sometimes incisions are made in the part affected; at other times red hot iron is laid upon it, to scorch and blister it, and sometimes they cover it with a plaster of fat.

In one of their villages the rising of a very stormy wind was attributed to our having changed our linen and clothes and the calm which commenced the following day they attributed to the same circumstance. Brother Schmelen having put on another waistcoat, they supposed the wind to have settled in consequence of the change. They do not like to be numbered, as they think it to be a token that death will soon take them away. On seeing the mist arise out of the sea, they believe that strangers are coming amongst them, and hold themselves in readiness. They are much afraid of an eclipse, as also of the meteor vulgarly called the falling star; they consider it a token of sickness amongst their cattle, and will drive them to another part, and beg of the star to spare them.

In their pastoral way of life they have not much work to require their attention; yet many of them have servants of the Damara nation to watch their cattle by day, and to bring them to the fold in the evening. Some of the Damaras are also employed amongst them as smiths, who make rings for their arms, assagays for their defence, and ornaments of copper for their ears, etc.

Some of the Namaquas make bamboos to contain their milk, and a few have small gardens for the purpose of raising tobacco, which they exchange with their neighbors. The women make mats for their houses, milk the cows, clean the grass-seed for food, and pound the bark with which their hair is powdered. When a hunting party is formed, the whole horde go out together, and, forming themselves into a large circle, they surround the place where it is expected that the animal will be found. The circle is then contracted, and all of them draw nearer to the object of their pursuit; on the rising up of the game each is ready for the attack, and a shower of assagays suddenly deprives him of life.

Some of them are kind to the sick, but the aged and infirm are often treated with cruelty. When a party are about to emigrate to some other part of the country, a small enclosure is made of bushes; and here, those who are unable to travel (perhaps an aged father and mother) are shut up; a sheep is generally left for their subsistence, which being consumed, they either die of hunger, or are devoured by the wild beasts.

At their funerals they practise no ceremonies. As soon as a person has ceased to breathe, his friends press the body, in order that the corpse may lie more compact. A small round hole is then scratched in the ground, and the corpse is placed in it, in a sitting posture; after which a pile of stones, to the height of four or five feet, is heaped upon it, to prevent any wild animals from taking it away. They are generally much alarmed at the thought of death, and when a family has lost one of its members, the house in which they dwelt is speedily removed to another situation.

They seem to have but little traffic; yet from the many iron bodkins which we saw amongst them, it is certain that they have some intercourse with the nations on the east. On inquiring from whom they had obtained those articles, they answered, "From the people where the sun comes up." It is evident that the natives cross the continent from east to west, and I doubt not but missionaries will find that course, and be able to unite, by a chain of various links, the missions to the Bechuanas with those of the Great Namaquas.[59]

This detailed account represents one of the earliest written records of the Nama. Any attempt to analyze the Namibian people should consider this account, as it relates many, although not all, of the practices and beliefs also to be found among other Namibian people.

Kido Witbooi led some of the Orlams from the Cape. Kido's successor was his son, Moses Witbooi. Then Hendrik Witbooi succeeded his father, Moses Witbooi. It should be noted that Afrikaner (Afrikander) also led the Afrikaners from the Cape with his brother Titus. Afrikaner's son, Jager Afrikaner, then took over the leadership. Jonker Afrikaner, Jager's son, followed him in leadership. Jonker is a contemporary of Chief Tjamuaha of the Herero. Jan Jonker Afrikaner was the son of Jonker, who in turn succeeded his father.

THE OVAMBO (AAWAMBO)[60]

The Ovambo straddle the present day frontiers between Angola and Namibia. Portugal and Germany split these people in 1890, with the result that two thirds of the Aakwanyama live in Angola and one third live in Namibia. Opinions on the origin of the Ovambo are conflicting. It is not known how long they lived in Namibia. Popular opinion is that the Ovambo came from the east sometime between the twelfth and seventeenth centuries. There are also other possibilities. One possibility is that they might have come from the northeast over the Zambezi and Okavango Rivers and trekked westwards. Second, they might have come from the north through Angola over the Kunene or between the Kunene and the Okavango Rivers. Some followed the rivers while others moved southwards parallel to the rivers. There is no answer yet to how they really came into the territory. It is also not proved that all came as a group. They may have come family by family or in individual clans. Nevertheless, they are part of the Bantu movement from the northeast to the southwest of Africa, according to the Bantu legends and myths.

The name "Ovambo" was probably given these people by their Herero neighbors. "Ovambo" is a collective name of eight (most people prefer seven) different tribes, each of which has its own language. They include Aakwanyama, Aakwambi, Aandonga, Aangandjera, Aambalantu, Aakwaluudhi, Aakolonkadhi, and "Aaunda" (those who live in Eunda).

The Ovambo themselves have several legends of their origin. One of these speaks about the three Ovambo ancestors: Mangundu, Kantene and Mungandjera. The second tells about Mangundu and his wife, who were created after Kalunga[61] (God) created all other things. Kalunga struck the termites' hill with a stick. A hole appeared in it. Kalunga commanded people to come out of the hill. Mangundu and his wife came out. They lived together at Otjimpolo (Oshimpolo). They bore two sons, Kanzi and Nangombe, and a girl. Kanzi got married and had a son called Mushindi, who later became a leader of the Aakwanyama (those who like meat). Nangombe's descendants became Aandonga, who settled in Ondonga. The third legend tells about a man, Noni, and a woman whom Kalunga brought forth out of the earth. They had three sons and a daughter called Janoni. One son was to take care of the cattle, another was charged with the care of the soil, while the third was responsible for the holy fire. Janoni became the ancestral mother. "This highly symbolic tale reflects the activities, the religion—Kalunga and the holy fire—and the matriarchal order of the Ovambos."[62] The fourth legend is a variation of the first one, which tells about the common ancestors of the Herero and Ovambo. It is about two brothers, Nangombe and Kadhu, the sons of Mangundu. Apparently the two brothers trekked southward from the north and journeyed south of the Zambezi until they reached the "Omumborombonga" tree somewhere in Ovamboland. It was at this tree they went their separate ways. Kadhu trekked further, first westward to the Kaokoveld and then southward to the central highlands of Namibia. Kadhu became the great ancestor of the Herero. Nangombe remained in Ovamboland and therefore was the Ovambo great ancestor.

The "Omumborombonga" tree is also known in the Herero legends of origin and connected to the Ovambo. It is also said that the Ovakango and the Ovambo migrated together from Central Africa. While the Ovambo moved westward, the Ovakavango remained on the banks of the Okavango River, evidently under the leadership of two sisters. The San people inhabited the regions of Okavangoland and Ovamboland long before these new Bantu immigrants.

As "Ovambo" is a collective term for the eight different tribes of Ovamboland, "Oshiwambo" is a collective term for their languages, namely, Oshikwanyama, Oshindonga, Otshikwambi, Oshingandjera, Oshimbalantu, Oshikwaluudhi, Oshikolokadhi, and Oshiunda (in Eunda).[63] These are all Bantu languages closely related, as Spanish, Portuguese and Italian are related. Their relationship to Herero is almost like that of English to Spanish.[64] Among the Ovambo lan-

guages only Oshikwanyama, Oshindonga and Otshikwambi are in
written form today. The Ovambo are matrilineal, i.e., the children
belong to the side of the mother and kingship is not inherited from
father to son, but rather from brother to brother or sister or someone
from the king's or queen's mother's side. Some tribes had and still
have kings (aakwaniilwa, or eehamba) and others had or still have
chiefs.

In the tribe where there is no king or queen, there are several chiefs
who by virtue of their work function the same way as those who are
under the king. Instead of the king, there is "The Chiefs' Council,"
which is the highest authority in that particular setting of the "nation" (oshigwana). One of the chiefs emerges, not necessarily
through election of any kind but according to nature and quality of
leadership capability, as a Paramount Chief—the one who is looked
upon in convening the Council to handle the "national" issues. This
particular chief, although not in strict terms, is the one to be con-
tacted first in times of crisis which call for drastic steps to be taken
without wasting time. Here follow the terms used for particular people:

1. Omukwaniilwa, Ohamba—King or Queen. Only those from the
   royal family.
2. Omunyekadhi. The wife of the king. She is never from the royal
   family and, therefore, she cannot give birth to kings or queens.
   One from a royal family has to marry outside the royal family.
3. Oshitenya. The husband of the queen. He, too, is not from the
   royal family. However, his children can become kings or queens.
4. Elenga Enene, Mwene gwOshikandjo. Chief, Senior Headman,
   or District-in-Charge. A district is a subdivision of "Oshilongo."
5. Elenga Eshona, Mwene gwOmukunda. Headman, Junior Headman, or Area-in-Charge. An area is a subdivision of "Oshikandjo" (District).

After the colonization of Namibia and elsewhere in Africa, those
who were known as kings were referred to as "Chiefs" as well. This
is incorrect. They are still known as kings (aakwaniilwa) in their territories.

The king is the ruler of the whole "nation" (Oshilongo). Oshilongo
is divided into several Iikandjo (singular: Oshikandjo). Each Oshikandjo is under the charge of the chief. Under the king there are usually several chiefs who time and again serve as the king's advisors or

The Social Organization of the Ovambo with the Ondonga Structure as an Example

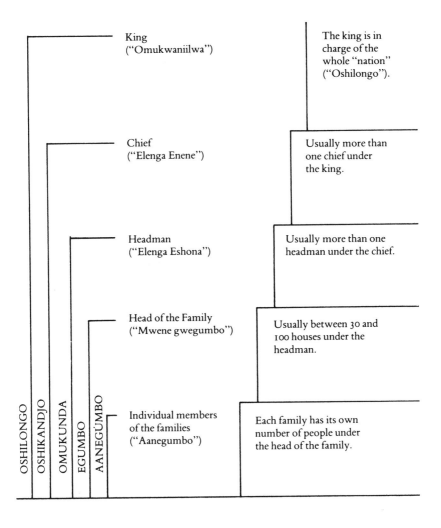

					King ("Omukwaniilwa")		The king is in charge of the whole "nation" ("Oshilongo").
					Chief ("Elenga Enene")		Usually more than one chief under the king.
					Headman ("Elenga Eshona")		Usually more than one headman under the chief.
					Head of the Family ("Mwene gwegumbo")		Usually between 30 and 100 houses under the headman.
OSHILONGO	OSHIKANDJO	OMUKUNDA	EGUMBO	AANEGÚMBO	Individual members of the families ("Aanegumbo")		Each family has its own number of people under the head of the family.

commanders of war. *Oshikandjo* is further subdivided into small areas or *Omikunda* (singular *Omukunda*). Each *Omukunda* is under the charge of a Headman (*Omunamukunda* or *Mwene gwomukunda*). Headmen in turn serve as advisors to the chiefs (*Aaniikandjo* or *Ooyene yiikanjo*; singular: *Omunashikandjo* or *Mwene gwoshikandjo*). Under the headman (*Omunamukunda*) there are several werfs or houses, usually between thirty and one hundred. As a general rule, each house is under the Head of the Family (*Omunegumbo* or *Mwene gwegumbo*), who is responsible for his/her households (*aanegumbo*) or individual members of the house.

All conflicts are handled from the bottom up in the social hierarchy. The king is the highest authority (a Supreme Court of Law) and therefore only a few extreme cases reach the "Supreme Court." Crimes and conflicts are considered accordingly at each level of the judicial pattern of the community. The king also functions as the judge, priest, and chief-in-command of the national army. In the king's palace a sacred fire is never allowed to die. In time of war, the king appoints a general who will take care of the firewood (*omukuluntu gwoshikuni*). However, there were priests besides the king whose advice was sought in matters of public importance and of common concern, such as rain. This was done by solemn embassy.

Economically, the Ovambo are agriculturists and animal herders. They supplement this with fishing, hunting, and gathering. They also have skills of basketry, pottery, woodworking and metalworking.

The Ovambo practices, as those of other Africans, were too complicated for the Europeans to understand, as pointed out in this quotation by Barbara Tyrrell:

Behaviour, manners and ethics are tribal and to sin against the interests of the tribe is sin indeed. There is no "absolute" in the sense of right and wrong and, therefore, no spiritual ideal to pursue. A crime, though it may even be murder, is no crime if it is in the interests of the tribe. . . . Many a religious teacher and many a European employer has found himself confused and frustrated because he has not been aware of this fundamentally different approach to, and interpretation of, truth and goodness.[65]

It is true that things are communally controlled and done in the interests of the community. It is also true that if individual interests were allowed to override the communal interests too much, it would be the destruction of the community and the promotion of fanatical individualism. Sin is conceived in practical terms rather than abstract terms. It is also the case that true or false, right or wrong, cannot be absolutized but remains a matter of convention. History has recorded "truths" which were later disproved as falsehoods. The Ovambo shies away from making anything absolute; to absolutize something is the business of the perfect agent. Such an agent is not an earthly phenomenon. It is fallacious for even a European who is dominated by individualism to be confused by what is taken as a "right murder" done for the sake of the community. The simple fact is that capital punishment is still practiced in Europe or in the so-called "civilized" countries. Wars and deadly weapons are made by these countries, all in the name of the community. In these and similar matters the ideals of the community rule decision-making. This same pattern is followed by all societies at all stages of development.

The earliest information about Ovamboland is derived from the Englishman Andrew Battles. In 1589, Battles was taken prisoner by the Portuguese in Brazil (South America) and brought to Angola. He was made to serve in the Portuguese colonial army and attained the rank of sergeant. However, Battles fled the army and was captured by the Jagga people, who in return used him in their forces. His service in Jagga military expeditions took him as far as Ovamboland in the south of present day Angola. Battles managed to escape from the Jagga after serving in their army for about a year and a half. This time he ended up in his native land, England.[66]

The second account of Ovamboland is to be found in the journals of Charles John Andersson, a Swedish naturalist who first used the name South West Africa; his colleague Frances Galton, an English explorer; and J. Allen, who visited King Nangolo dhAmutenya of Ondonga in 1851 for eight days. Their purpose was to reach the Kunene River through Ovamboland, but King Nangolo did not give them a passage. These explorers and hunters from the south were followed by the Rhenish missionaries Hugo Hahn, Rath and Green (the trader), who visited Ovamboland in 1857 and 1866. In the meantime, Jonker Afrikaner, Chief of the Nama, visited Ondonga in 1858 and 1860. These southern visitors introduced guns into Ovamboland.

Upon the establishment of German colonial rule in Namibia, Ovamboland was left alone for a while because the Germans lacked the necessary army to combat the formidable Ovambo forces. When King Haimbili (1805–58) of Uukwanyama sought European trade in the 1850s, Shishaama Shandunge, a poet-prophet, opposed him, predicting that Haimbili's allowing the white traders to come would be followed by their suppression.

When other indigenous "nations" were being crushed both to their north and to their south, the Ovambo kings rushed to the aid of their neighbors against the Portuguese in the north and the Germans in the south. The Herero appealed for reinforcement from Ovambo kings. In 1904 King Nehale lyaMpingana of Ondonga east (Oshitambi) rushed to the Herero's aid. With about five hundred men, Nehale attacked the Germans at the Namutoni fort. The Germans were well-fortified and as a result the Ovambo lost about 108 men. In the north, King Mandume gaNdemufayo of Uukwanyama had been fighting the Portuguese since 1911. After the surrender of the German troops to the South African forces in 1915, two British Commissioners resided at Ondangwa and Onamakunde in the same year. This action provoked King Mandume even more against the Portuguese. Mandume lost heavily. Ruth First reports the casualties on both sides as follows:

The Portuguese had mustered a force of 1,200 men, and suffered a hundred casualties. Between 4,000 and 5,000 Africans had been killed. The Portuguese announced that no prisoners had been taken during the action, that the bodies of the "natives" which lay heaped before the trenches had been sprinkled with petrol and burned.[67]

Struck heavily by the Portuguese, Mandume was forced to submit to the South African forces' "protection." However, Lieutenant C. H. L. Hahn (the grandson of C. H. Hahn, the missionary), who was in command of the South African troops and who later became Commissioner (Shongola) at Ondangwa, Ovamboland, ordered Mandume to surrender. In reply Mandume vowed: "I will fight till my last bullet is spent." The following quotation shows that the Portuguese and the South Africans had their own aim—the aim of dealing with Mandume.

The Portuguese and South Africans settled their dispute over the undefined border by tracing a line through the midst of the Ovambo people. But Mandume and his people refused not to cross the artificial border and they were attacked by the Europeans at Ondjiva. However, the king and his bodyguard escaped and allegedly committed suicide. According to a popular account, his head was later cut off as a trophy by the South Africans and taken in triumph to Windhoek where it was buried in a park which no African is still allowed to enter.[68]

In 1932, the South African troops took military action against King Iipumbu yaTshilongo of Uukwambi, who, according to the Administrator's report of 1922, had been described as the one who is reluctant "to submit to the authority of the Commissioner." His palace was bombarded and he himself taken hostage and exiled from his people to Okavango. Later Iipumbu came back to Ovamboland and lived in Uukwanyama. One is, therefore, tempted to agree with Tötemeyer in the following observations:

The period 1915–60 was characterized by stagnation and indirect white administration, which was anxious to subject the traditional order to the minimum of innovations and outside influences and would brook no move by the traditional community to question the authority of indirect white control or to abolish it. In fact no initiative was shown by the authorities in transforming traditional administrative institutions and adapting them to a modern framework, which would necessarily have made them more effective.[69]

The indirect white administration never ended. The year 1960 began with the "inauguration" of the national spirit under several African political parties as well as with the "Odendaal Commission" appointed by the South African State President in 1962. In 1964 the commission recommended the division of Namibia into "homelands" and made Ovamboland one of the ten "homelands." In 1973 Ovamboland received its own administration and flag with King Uushona Shiimi as Chief Minister of Ovamboland, contrary to the Ovambo election of the same year. Up to the present, the situation has not improved, with Ovamboland under the martial law imposed in the region in 1978 and heavy South African troops patroling day and night ready to shoot to kill.

The Lutheran missionaries from Finland have been tirelessly laboring among the Ovambo people since 1870. The Roman Catholic Church, the Anglicans and other denominations followed later and have a large following as well.

The Kings of Ovamboland*

Ondonga

Name	Years of Reign	Place of Palace
Nembulungo lyaNgwedha	1650–?	
Mbwenge gUule (shindongo shaNamutenya)	?–1800	Ombalamumbwenge
Nangombe yaMvula (Kajone, Mulingi)	1800–1810	Ombalamumbwenge
Nembungu lyAmutundu	1810–20	Oshamba (Iinenge)

Nangolo dhAmuteny (Nembungu's nephew)	1820–57	Ondonga
Shipanga shAmukwiita	1857–58	
Shikongo sha Kalulu	1858–74	Ondjumba (Omandongo)
Kambonde kaNankwaya	1874–83	Onamumgundo
Iitana yaNekuyu	1883–84	
Kambonde kaMpingana	1884–1909	Okaloko
(Nehale lyaMpinga, Ondonga East	1885–1908	Oshitambi, Onayena)
Kambonde kaNgula	1909–12	Ontananga?
Nambala (Martin Elifas) yaKadhikwa	1912–42	Okaloko
Sheepo shaNamene (Eino Johannes Kambonde)	1942–60	
Martin Ashikoto	1960–67?	
Paulus Elifas	1967–70	Oneputa
Filemon Elifas	1970–75	
Immanuel Elifas	1975–	Olukonda

Ombalantu

They had no kings, but only chiefs. Some of these chiefs are:

Name	Years of Reign
Kampaku kaHuhwa	1810–35
Mvula yEposhi	
Amuhelo gwaKalipi	
Iishitile yUukahanona	
iita yIitewa	
Eyelu lyElago	
Amvula yAlweendo	
Shigwedha shAlweendo	

In 1915, the South African government created a tribal council of four chiefs.

Uukwanyama

Name	Years of Reign	Place of Palace
Kambungu		Onambambi/ Onehula
Shitenhu		Oshiteve
Kavonga KaHaindongo	ca. 1600	Ondjiva
Kawengeko		Ondjiva
Kapuleko kaVandja (Mushindi waKanhene)	1650–90	Ondjiva
Heita yaAmuvale	1690–?	Ondjiva
Hautolonde yaVandja	ca. 1755–60	Ondjiva
Mutota gwaHaipiya	1760–66	Ondjiva
Shimbilinga shaNailambi	1766–1806	Ondjiva

Haihambo yaMukwanhuli	1806–7	Ondjiva
Hamangulu yaNaivala	1807–11	Ondjiva
Haimbili yaHaufiku	1811–58	Ondjiva
Haikukutu yaShinangolo	1858–59	Ondjiva
Sheefeni shaHamukuyu	1859–62	Ondjiva
Mweshipandeka shaSha- ningika	1862–82	Ondjiva
Namhadi yaMweyihanyeka	1882–85	
Ueyulu waHedimbi	1885–1904	Ondjiva
Nande yaHedimbi	1904–11	Omukumbwaimbi
Mandume gaNdemufayo	1911–17	Ondjiva

From 1917 until today the Aakwanyama have been governed by chiefs. In lieu of kingship, South Africa created a tribal council of eight chiefs.

Uukwambi

Name	Years of Reign	Place of Palace
Nuuyoma/Neyema/ Nakwedhi	ca. 1650–1700	
Atshipala tshaNakwedhi	1700–1750	
Nakantu kaNakwedhi	1750–80	
Nuukata waShinga	1780–1800	
Iilonga haNyango	1800–1820	
Tshikesho tshaNyango	1820–30	
Tshikongo tshaNyango	1830–40	
Nuuyoma wIipumbu	1840–60	Iino
Iipmubu haNangaku	1860–70	
Tshikesho tshEelu	1870–75	
Negumbo lyaKandenge	1875–1907	
Iipumbu yaTshilongo	1908–32	Uungwelu/Oma- pona/Onashiku

Iipumbu was the last king of Uukwambi. He was replaced by the council of four chiefs created by South Africa in 1932, with Silas Iipumbu as senior chief.

Ongandjera

Name	Years of Reign
Nangombe yaMangundu	
Amatundu gaNima	
Nkandi yAmwaalwa	
Niita yIitula (a woman, Nkandi's sister)	
Shaanika shaShiimi	
Amunyela gwaShaningwa	ca. ?–1856
Nakahwa kaShivute (a woman)	ca. 1856–57
Ekandjo lyaKadhila	1857–63
Sheya shUushona	1863–78

Iiyambo yIileka	1878–87
Shaanika shaNashilongo	1887–1930
Sheya shaAmukwa	1930–36
Shanika shIipinge	1936–48
Uushona waShiimi	1948–72
Jafet Malenga	1972–?
J. M. Munkundi	?–

Uukwaluudhi

Name	Years of Reign	
Shikwa shAmupindi		(Kayambu)
Nashilongo shIikombo		
Nakakwiila kAmunyela		
Amukwa gwAmunyela		
Niilenge yaShipuula		
Uushona wEndjala		
Shikongo shIipinge	?–1903	
Niilenge yAmukwa	1903–8	
Iita yaNadhitoke	1908–9	
Mwaala gwaNashilongo	1909–60	
Shikongo Taapopi	1960–	

Eunda and Uukolonkadhi

Since about 1700 these two "nations" (*iilongo*) have not had kings or chiefs. They had several autonomous leaders or headmen and leaders of families who did not have a unified, central leadership like other tribes. However, as time passed, they too organized themselves in a similar federal system with prominent headmen. When South Africa moved into the areas, it appointed eight people as senior headmen—five of them in Uukolonkadhi and two in Eunda. Two of these people were made "chiefs."

O kalongo (i.e., Okalongo kUudhano)

In the olden days Okalongo was also ruled by prominent leaders. It was almost like a separate tribal area. Uudhano waNgwali yaShoombe was one of those leaders. Other tribes went to Okalongo to get commodities in times of famine or droughts. Because of the plenty of the Okalongo, the Aandonga, Aakwanyama, Aakwambi and Aangandjera invaded the Okalongo people and defeated them. These people were then taken along to these "nations" (*iilongo*) as prisoners of war. Today Okalongo is generally considered part of the Uukwanyama tribe.

THE SAN

The San or Ju (ie., "people") people, who used to be called by the pejorative designation "Bushmen" by the colonialists, are probably the earliest inhabitants of Namibia. Nearly all of southern Africa has been inhabited by these people for about twelve to fifteen thousand years.[70] It is generally agreed that the San came from the north to southern Africa, including Namibia. Their rock paintings are found in Tanzania, Uganda, southern Sudan, and other parts of tropical East and East-Central Africa. Estimation is that there are probably not more than sixty thousand of them in the whole of southern Africa today.

The San are so distinctive in appearance that one can easily distinguish them from all other Africans. Although they are not pygmies, they are short, with an average height of about sixty inches. Their limbs are well-shaped and their hands and feet are small. Their skin is yellow to yellow-brown. Their hair is sparsely grown, assuming a "peppercorn" appearance.

The head is mesaticephalic, high in the crown; the face is orthognathous and flat, with prominent cheek-bones, very flat nose, and bulging forehead. The eyes are narrow, often slightly oblique, the lobe may be absent from the ear. The usual forward curvature of the lower end of the spine is exaggerated, making the buttocks specially prominent, and with the women there is often that considerable accumulation of fat on the buttocks and thighs to which is given the name steatopygy.[71]

Linguistically there are several languages of each tribe among the San. The main tribes are the !Khung, Heikum, Ovangongolo, Aayelele, Auen, Naron, Tannekwe, Hukwe, Galikwe, Barkwengo, and Masarwa (Tati), who speak languages similar in click sounds to Damara-Nama such as Ju (Kung or !Xu), Ta'a, Kwi, Xû, Hai-n// um, etc.

Traditionally the San lived as hunters and gatherers grouped in small bands of thirty to one hundred people. "A number of these bands, united by a common name and language, form a tribe, but the tribe has little importance in regulating social life, and the bands are completely independent and autonomous."[72] Each tribe recognizes another tribe's hunting territory. Any intruder in a tribal territory can be attacked with bow and poisoned arrows without any warning. It is on such territories that each tribe hunts for animals. When animals are scarce, the San depend solely on food of the veld, which includes veld "onions," different bulbs, tubers, roots, nuts, a variety of fruits, insects, lizards, some kinds of snakes, and whatever the eyes are able to see and the stomachs strong enough to take in and process without harm. The San do not practice agriculture or keep or tame animals, except dogs. They hunt almost all kinds of animals except those which are similar to human beings or which eat human flesh or serve as valuable resources of food in times of need. Such animals are: the baboon, the hyena, and the little mole, respectively. The little mole collects wild "onions" and other bulbs, tubers and roots during winter time and stores them in the ground for its own use. This "storehouse" of the mole becomes also at times a valuable "storage" for the people (San).[73]

The San's respect of nature leads them to the point where they do not exploit the forests by cutting down the trees and building beautiful houses for themselves. Their shelters for centuries have been made of a few branches and twigs, mostly of a temporary nature and dwelling. Although this life of the San is superficially seen as simple and less civilized, the San are sophisticated and more civilized in their way of behavior and respect of life as a whole. They can go without food and water for amazingly long periods on their hunting trips. They are never wasteful in hunting, but kill only as much as they need. In general, the San are armed with "razor-sharp instincts and unsurpassable know-how of the elemental mechanisms of nature."[74] Part of their sophistication is seen in rock paintings. There are some similarities between the rock paintings in the hills of southern Africa and those found in middle Europe. In the course of thousands of years, the San might have migrated from Europe through the Strait of Gibraltar to Africa, "for their skeletal remains and their paintings and etchings are widespread from the cape to East and North Africa."[75]

These paintings are . . . outstanding as they are in their exquisite design, simply of configuration, and wealth of natural expression. Several of these paintings point to contact with ancient Mediterranean civilisations. More recent ones portray contacts with the first White settlers in the subcontinent; but the vast majority breathe the aura of distant yester-years—timeless mysteries expressed in shape and colour.[76]

Above all, the San are great hunters, good painters and sculpturers, music-makers with the sense of music, actors, gentle, harmless, affectionate, skillful, good dancers, inspired storytellers, instinctive artists, and people with intimate knowledge of nature. Although they permit polygamy, they are mostly monogamous. They have an intense fear of incest. They can only marry across the bands, because marriage within the band is prohibited. Grown up brothers and sisters should avoid company as well as mothers-in-law and sons-in-law.

Upon the arrival of other people in the region, the process of displacing the San from their traditional hunting grounds began. "The arrival of Europeans . . . sped up the process, and the Boer-organized commandos had virtually exterminated the San in South Africa by the end of the 19th century."[77] As a result, today most of the San are found in Namibia and a few in Botswana, Zimbabwe, Zambia, and Angola. If Diego Cao took any Namibians with him from Cape Cross to Portugal (it was a popular Portuguese instruction to capture a few local people whenever they could and take them to Portugal with the idea that these "barbarians" would learn "civilization") in 1484, they must have been either the San or Nama or Herero who were living not very far from the coast.

With the onset of industrialization and new national boundaries, the San's traditional mode of life has also been disturbed. They are no longer free to move around and hunt. A "homeland" in the east of Namibia has been set aside for them like any other ethnic group in the country. The "Advisory Board for Bushmen" was established in October 1976. Already in 1879, Schröder, a Rhenish missionary, tried to form contacts for mission work among the Kalahari San. Heinrich Veder also grouped some San at Gaub in 1911, but it did not flourish until 1930 when the Rhenish Missionary Society intensified its mission to the San.

There is a lesson to learn from these almost forgotten people of Africa. The San do whatever is possible to avoid quarreling and jealousy among themselves. Sharing with one another is imperative in their culture. This attitude of sharing and cooperation helped them to survive extreme dangers of hunger and drought in years past. Their humane nature and the way they share even the little for the sake of "saving" others to survive should be the best model for all greedy people. Life is not necessarily precious and joyful only when there is plenty and strength, but is more enjoyable if others see and recognize the presence of others and share even the crumbs. Poverty is not always the lack of plenty, and affluence is not always the presence of material possessions. What is more humane is the equitable sharing of whatever material is available, irrespective of its amount.

The San languages are characterized by click sounds produced with an ingressive air stream when the tongue is drawn sharply away from various points of articulation on the roof of the mouth. The four clicks used in !Kung appear as follows:

/   Dental click, as in /Xai/xai, /Du/da (in spoken English this sound denotes a mild reproach, written "tsk, tsk")

≠   Alveolar click, as in ≠To//gana, ≠Toma

!   Alveopalatal click, as in !Kung, /Ti!kai

//   Lateral click, as in ≠To//gana, //wama (in spoken English this sound is used in some dialects to urge on a horse)

Other features of the San orthography that should be noted include:

⁻   Nasalization, as in /twā

__   Pressing, as in maa

'   Glottal stop, as in ts'i

"   Glottal flap, as in //"xa (mongongo)

Tone markers: low, as in !gwe‿; high, as in !gu⁻

For the nonlinguist, San words may be pronounced by simply dropping the click. For example, ≠To//gana may be read Togana, /Ti!kai may be read Tikai.

The Source for this information is Richard Borshay Lee, *The !Kung San: Men, Women, and Work in a Foraging Society* (New York: Cambridge University Press, 1979), p. xxv.

THE TSWANA

We do not have much information on the Tswana people. What we do know is that the Tswana of Namibia are related to those of the Republic of Botswana who formerly occupied much of northern South Africa, including the Transvaal and the Orange Free State. Linguistically, they are related to the Sotho. They are patrilineally organized and practice farming and agriculture.

The Tswana of Botswana include the Bakwena, Bamangwato, Bakgathla, Batawana, Barolong, Bathlaping, Bangwaketse, and Bahurushe. It is possible that most of these tribes are also represented in the Namibian Tswana. Those of Botswana are also patrilineal and pastoral.

The Tswana community in Namibia is very small and lives mostly around Aminuis together with some Herero. The Roman Catholic Church started mission work among the Tswana at Aminuis in 1902 and at Epukiro in 1903. In 1926 the Rhenish Mission began work among them at Epukiro. Since 1908 the Rhenish had done some mission work at Gobabis, however.

THE SETTLERS

We are using the term "settlers" to refer to those people who are not of African origin or do not have native African blood in them. These people call themselves "whites" as a term opposed to "blacks," although in some Namibian languages they are known as *aatiligane* (i.e., "red people"). The white people came to Namibia as hunters, traders, missionaries, farmers, officials, copper and diamond searchers, and soldiers.

The white population is predominantly comprised of the Boers— people of Dutch origin, or Afrikaaners as they call themselves, and people of German origin. Those of British origin comprise a smaller number, mostly from South Africa. There are also other white folks, either of American or other European countries by origin. Although a good number of whites can in principle today be regarded as Namibian citizens, many of them are expatriates whose territorial base is still South Africa.

The first European settlers,[78] mostly Germans, came to Namibia in the 1840s under the auspices of the London Missionary Society. However, the two major periods of great German immigration into Namibia were, first, between 1870 and 1915 and, second, after World War II. The total German population in 1903 was only 4,700. The Boers entered Namibia on a large scale after the South African invasion of Namibia in 1915.

Today, each white group speaks its own language, *i.e.,* Afrikaans for the Boers, German and English for the Germans and British respectively. However, Afrikaans is spoken as a *lingua franca*. It is very interesting to note that despite the differences in origins, cultures and languages, the whites are treated as one race, unlike the Africans (blacks), who are treated as separate "indigenous peoples."

In Namibia whites enjoy political and economic privilege and domination. The introduction of the European custom of selling or leasing land brought a serious misunderstanding between Africans and European settlers. The land acquisition by the whites, however "legal" or "fair" it was, was contrary to African traditional customs. For Africans, the land belongs to all people, both the living and the dead, and is therefore inalienable. It cannot be purchased by anyone.

One of the major reasons for the Herero and Nama rebellion against the Germans was the sense of injustice and disaffection caused by the white settlement and their hunger for land. The Chilembwe rising of 1915 in Malawi and the Mau Mau conflict with settlers in Kenya from 1952 are examples of the violence caused by the presence of white settlements on "peoples' lands."

The same sense of grievance over alienation of land inevitably rubbed off on missionaries also. They too had settled on tribal land, often of best quality, and their farms were always the best in the area. Africans were quick to notice as well that they offered special ministrations to white farmers and enjoyed their society. Not surprisingly therefore, missionaries were identified with settlers in African eyes, thereby creating one more factor in the growing climate of tension.[79]

Today the white Namibians enjoy not only political and economic rights and privileges, but also all other things, including health and education. In 1903 only 3.6 percent of the land was under white settlers. But the living conditions of blacks and whites today can be statistically compared this way:

Category	Blacks	Whites
Population	90%	10%
Arable land allotted	10%	90%
Per capita income	124 rand	3,000 rand
Per capita amount spent on health services	5.40 rand	270 rand
Per capita amount spent on education	214 rand	1,500 rand
Ratio of wages paid in mines	5% (1 rand)	100% (20 rand)

About 50 percent of the black population has lived under martial law since 1978. Black women suffer a double injustice; they earn less than either black men or white women. Malnutrition deprives 163 out of 1,000 black children of life in their first years as compared to 21.6 out of 1,000 white children.[80]

The way of life among white Namibians is contrary to what Rhoodie praised them for: [they] "as bearers of Western Civilization . . . introduced the rule of law, educational services, welfare and Christianity."[81] Christianity without justice is false. Civilization under the rule of an iron hand is invalid. The whites in Namibia should realize that it is high time for them to know that they are no longer

Europeans, but Namibians who, together with other Namibian races, should join with the Namibian cause, not as superiors but as equals working for the improvement of socio-economic and socio-political conditions and for the creation of a new future culture.

Church affiliation among the whites is found in most major denominations in the country, such as Roman Catholic, Anglican, Lutheran and Dutch Reformed.

THE PORTUGUESE NAVIGATORS

The desire for riches in Europe took momentum during the collapse of the Eastern Empire with the fall of Constantinople in 1453. Constantinople was a bridge between East and West. It was a trading center for the wondrous products of the East. The fall of Constantinople to the Arabs blocked the door to the East and necessitated that a new route be found. Already in the eleventh century when the Christian Crusaders brought back Eastern goods, especially spices from China and India, the desire for more riches combined with the curiosity of exploring new areas influenced kings and sailors. Many people were encouraged by the printing of Marco Polo's stories of his adventures and travels in far and strange lands.[82] Western Europe was now preoccupied with establishing new routes to the East.

It was the tiny country of Portugal which took the lead in embarking on exploration. During the 1400s Prince Henry of Portugal, who had great interest in the sea and who might have obtained much information about Africa through Ceuta, the Portuguese captured fortress port of Morocco, began a school for seamen. This school was comprised of sailors, astronomers, ship-builders, cartographers, instrument-makers, and other hired experts of the sea. Prince Henry's interest in the sea brought him a new name: Henry the Navigator.

Beginning in the 1420s, Henry the Navigator sent out small, regular expeditions to Lagos to explore the African west coast.[83] In the mid-1400s the Portuguese ships brought thousands of slaves from western Africa. Some of these slaves were Christianized and versed in the Portuguese language. They were used in Africa as interpreters in further expeditions and slave trading. When Prince Henry died in 1460, the pace of African explorations slackened. After the 1470s the Portuguese desire again revived. Fernando Po reached some islands near the mouth of the Niger in 1471. In 1481 Prince John II became the king of Portugal. He was regarded as "a competent geographer and an enthusiast for discovery."[84] Soon, at Crown expense, John II pursued African coastal explorations. Among his distinguished captains were Diogo Cao (Diego Cao, Cam, or Jakobus Canus), and Bartholomeu Diaz (Dias).

Diogo Cao (ca. 1450–86) was the leading Portuguese navigator, explorer and mariner of his country.[85] Cao left Portugal in the spring of 1482 and sailed around the Gulf of Guinea. He erected several limestone pillars—*padroes*—along the west coast of Africa which "served as landmarks, as assertions of Portuguese authority, and as symbols of Christianity."[86] In 1483 Cao reached the mouth of the Congo. He navigated southward from the Congo, where he left some of his crew. On his return to the Congo, Cao took Congolese hostages with him to Portugal. On his second voyage, Cao sailed further south until he reached Cape Cross (Cabo do Padrao) in 1484[87] on the west coast of Namibia. This was eight years before Christopher Columbus set foot on the islands[88] of the Americas on October 12, 1492. Until that time Namibia was still a land of "fable and mystery" to the Europeans. At Cape Cross Cao erected a cross, which was taken to Germany in 1893 and can be found today in Berlin,[89] bearing King John II's arms and this inscription:

Since the creation of the world 6684 years have passed and since the birth of Christ 1484 and so the illustrious King John has ordered this pillar to be erected here by Diego Cao, his knight.[90]

Christianity and trade were connected by the Portuguese. This is the way Vasco da Gama put it: "I seek Christians and spices."[91] In 1486 Diogo Cao returned again to Portugal. Despite Cao's contribution to Portuguese navigation—he covered 1,450 miles[92] on his voyages along the African coast—his later life is not known. Presumably he took another voyage in 1486 and died somewhere off the Namibian coast.

As the records make no further reference to C. [Cão], and as a gathering of scientists assembled at Badajoz in 1524 declared of him *en otro viage desdel diche Monte-negro pasé à Sierra Parda, donde murió* ('on another voyage he went past the Black Mountain to the Parda Mountain, where he died'), it can be regarded as almost certain that C. [Cão] did indeed die off the coast of South West Africa."[93]

Diogo Cao's successor was another capable captain, Bartholomeu Diaz (Dias, ca. 1450–1500), who led expeditions to the southernmost tip of Africa. Diaz left Lisbon in 1487.[94] In December 1487 Diaz reached the area of Walvis Bay and Angra Pequena (Lüderitz— "Cabo de Volta," "Angra das Ilheus," "Angra das Voltas" or "S. Cristovao"). Captain Diaz sailed further south around the tip of Africa until he reached the Bay of Cows ("Sao Bras"—Mossel Bay) in 1488 before he saw and bypassed the Cape of Good Hope. On his way back to Angra Pequena, where he left one of his three vessels, Diaz found the "Cape of Storms," which he named thus because it was found during a storm. Later, King John II of Portugal renamed "Cabo Tormentoso" (Cape of Storms) the "Cape of Good Hope" in anticipation of the coming discovery of the route to the Orient. Today it is known as Cape Town. At Angra Pequena Diaz erected the usual Portuguese *padraos,* whose fragments are today in the Windhoek museum.[95] Diaz, the first white person to reach the southern tip of Africa, returned to Portugal in December 1488. He died in 1500 in a great storm of the south Atlantic while commanding one of thirteen vessels sent out by Manuel I for the Sofalan enterprise. Four of the ships were destroyed in this storm, but the rest went on as far as the Brazilian coast.

About ten years later, another Portuguese captain, Vasco da Gama (1462–1524), ordered by King Dom Manuel to be commander-in-chief of four vessels and accompanied by his brother Paulo da Gama and Nicolau Coelho, left Portugal in July 1497 and sailed around the Cape of Good Hope. In March 1498 Da Gama reached Mozambique. It was not until May 20, 1498 that he arrived in Calcutta, India.

Until the Portuguese reached India, the Far East had been known to Europeans mainly through the accounts of thirteenth-century Franciscan missionaries, such as Carpini and William of Rubruck, who had visited the dominions of the Tartar Khanas, and of that incomparable traveller and observer, Marco Polo.[96]

Although Da Gama is not mentioned as ever landing on the Namibian coast, his voyage is worth mentioning because he continued where Diaz left off.

Da Gama was the first to explore from the Fish River to Sofala. He opened to Europeans the sea route to India, the discovery of which brought wealth to the crown of Portugal and led to European domination in the East. His visits to Sofala, Mozambique and Kilwa in 1502 prepared the way for the establishment of Portuguese forts in these centres in 1505 and 1507, these forts being the first European settlements to be found in southern Africa. But Da Gama's brutalities provoked the opposition of the Moslem world, and handicapped the establishment of diplomatic and commercial relations.[97]

On his return to Portugal in 1499, the king honored him with a royal title: "Lord of the conquest, navigation and commerce of Ethiopia, Arabia, Persia and India."[98] In 1502 Da Gama was sent back to India, where he returned the following year. Joao III sent Da Gama on another voyage in 1524, to India, but three months later Da Gama died at Cochin, India, and his body later brought back to Portugal.

In 1500 Pero Alverez Cabral, another Portuguese, followed Da Gama's route to the East. Caught in a storm, Cabral was blown off course and found himself in South America instead. He claimed South America as a possession of the Portuguese king. However, he did eventually manage to reach the East. His voyage was the second Portuguese fleet to India. Cabral established a factory at the port of Cochin.

All these expeditions opened up not only the route to the Orient, but also an entrance to future colonizations of new lands to accommodate the European population boom by emigrating some people to these far countries. "Eight years later the Portuguese sacked Kilwa and Mombasa. For more than a hundred years they treated the Indian Ocean as if it were a Portuguese lake."[99] Gasper (Gaspar) Vega (Veca) is another Portuguese who visited the coast of Namibia in 1534.[100]

Despite the "discovery" of the Namibian west coast by the Portuguese, none of these newcomers could stand the "hostile giant" (the Namib Desert) and thus never penetrated the interior of Namibia. Namibia was impenetrable until over two hundred years later, when two ways to intrude into it were found, from the south across the Orange River and from the east via Botswana or from the north.[101]

THE EXPLORERS, HUNTERS AND TRADERS

Exploration of Namibia got underway only after whites had settled South Africa two hundred years after the first Portuguese explorers. As Ruth First puts it:

Except for occasional landings during the next few centuries, with cursory glances at the country beyond; whale and seal catching, barter between ship's crews and Namas along the coast; and a small ship repair at Angra Pequena, South West Africa remained untouched by White men. When they entered the country at last in any numbers and for any length of time, it was overland, from South Africa.[102]

But this quotation cannot be understood unless we know a bit about the settlement at the Cape Colony by the Europeans.

From the beginning of the seventeenth century, ships of Dutch and English companies, formed from the 1590s to tap the wealth of the East, began to call regularly at the Cape to stock up with the fresh meat and greens necessary to ward off that scourge of European mariners to the East, scurvy. The earlier Portuguese sailors had tended to avoid the cape on their eastward journey on account of its capricious storms and apparently equally capricious inhabitants . . . with their sturdier vessels and different sea routes, the Dutch, British and to some extent the French, found the Cape a useful half-way house.[103]

Therefore, on April 6, 1652 a Dutchman, Jan Van Riebeeck, and his staff of about 120 servants of the Dutch East India Company arrived at the Cape of Good Hope "to establish a refreshment station, where fresh fruit and vegetables could be grown by its servants, and meat bartered from the local inhabitants."[104] By 1679 there were about six hundred white people in the Cape. This number had increased to nearly one thousand by 1694 due to the fact that white orphaned girls were sent there to meet the needs of white men plus the arrival in the Cape Colony in 1688 of 160 French Huguenots who fled France in the midst of religious persecutions. Ten years later the number of whites in the Cape had doubled, including those of German, French, Dutch, Swedish, Danish and Walloons backgrounds.[105] It was from this community setting that later explorations into the interior of Namibia were carried out both overland and by sea.

In 1670 a small exploration vessel, the "Grundel," was dispatched from the Cape to explore the coast of Namibia. It landed at Lüderitz Bay. Another ship, the "Bode" from the Cape, followed in 1677 with Captain Theodoor Wobma as its commander.[106] Its crew was repulsed by the Namibians at the mouth of the Kuiseb River. "An attempt to barter for cattle with them ended in misunderstanding and suspicion, and the Namas drove the landing party from Namibian soil."[107]

In 1738 William van Wyk and other Boers organized a secret overland expedition from the Cape Colony in an attempt to establish trade relationships with the Namibians. These Boers were surprised to learn that Pieter de Bruyan, another white man, preceded them into Namibia.

It was not until 1760 that Jacobus Coetzee, farmer and hunter, crossed the Gariep River (the Great River), which was renamed the Orange River in 1779 after the House of Orange by Colonel R. J. Gordon.[108] Coetzee trekked northward as far as Warmbad, Bunsenberg, and Rietfontein. On his return to the Cape Colony, he reported that African tribes (probably the Herero) had many cattle in Namibia. Coetzee also brought back "the hide and copper ore" to the Cape.

Another expedition to Namibia took place in 1761 under the leadership of Hendrik Hop, who was also joined by Coetzee and other Boer farmers.

After passing the "warm bath" [Warmbad] on 5 October, the trek reached Rietfontein on 11 October. The journey was then continued to the east of the Great Karasberg range as far as the Xamob River, a tributary of the Great Fish River. From here C. [Coetzee], Pieter Marais and Andries Greef were sent to reconnoitre the territory in a westerly direction, their trek taking another ten days. They returned with information about the Herero, Bergdamara, and Tswana, but, as they found the water supply inadequate and the terrain too difficult, the trek turned back in the neighbourhood of modern Grundorn (26° 85' S.).[109]

Another expedition to Namibia was that of the Cape Governor, Simon van der Stel, in 1762. H. J. Wilar crossed the Orange River in 1778 and lived for about two years in Namibia. He returned to the Cape in 1779. Wikar wrote many things about Namibia. He was probably the first to describe the country at that time. The explorer Willem van Reenen reached Modderfontein (Keetmanshoop) in 1791. The following year Van Reenen and Pieter Brandt reached the neighborhood of Rehoboth, and Brandt continued until he reached the Swakop River. Pieter Pienaar, who came by sea in a vessel called "Meermin," landed at Walvis Bay and explored the valley of Swakopmund in 1793.

Up to the mid-nineteenth century, the northern region of Namibia had been unexplored. In 1850 an Englishman and cousin of Charles Darwin, Francis Galton (1822–1911), landed in Walvis Bay together with an English-Swede, Charles J. Andersson (1827–67), with the aim to explore Namibia. Galton, Andersson and J. Allen decided to go to the Kunene River through Ovamboland in 1851. They met some Ovambo men in Damaraland (Hereroland),[110] numbering over twenty at Otjikango. These Ovambo were under the leadership of "Chikorongo-onkompe."[111] They came to trade with the Damara

(Herero).[112] On their way back to Ovamboland they were joined by other Ovambo men, and the group was combined with that of the explorers, including some Damara women and their children, to Ovamboland. On May 23, 1851 Galton counted them:

I counted in our caravan 86 Damara women, nearly half of whom had yelling babies on their backs, and 10 Damara men. Our party consisted of 14, and the Ovampo [Ovambo] of 24; making 170 souls in all; 206 head of horned cattle were driven along, independently of my own, and were the result of Ovampo [Ovambo] barter; and of these three-fourths were cows or heifers.[113]

On their way to Ovamboland the group came to Otjikoto Lake after they had passed Orujo Lake, which is smaller than Otjikoto. Then they reached Etosha and eventually arrived in Ondonga, Ovamboland, where they were fairly treated after the king gave the explorers a "visa" to enter his territory. King Nangolo dhAmutenya took two to three days before he would see these foreigners, as a way to humble them and to allow them officially to graze their oxen. When the king "saw" the explorers and welcomed them officially, the explorers were allowed to sell their goods among the Ondonga people (Aandonga). Galton and his companions felt uneasy about staying longer and wanted to leave soon.

We all felt uncomfortable. I never for a moment expected any attack from the Ovampo [Ovambo], but I had considerable misgivings that they purposely intended to keep my oxen in low condition that I might be less independent. Ondonga is a difficult way to get away from . . . a quick retreat I hardly know how I should have done it. . . . The country is remarkably uniform, intersected with paths, and quite destitute of natural features to guide us. It is also slightly undulating, enough so to limit the view to a mile or two ahead.[114]

The explorers left Ovamboland on June 13, 1851 and went back to the central-south of Namibia because King Nangolo refused them a passage to the Kuene River.

After the Ovamboland visit, Galton and Andersson went eastward and reached Tounobis. In 1852 Andersson, without Galton, reached Lake Ngami. In between, Andersson went to Europe. When he came back, Andersson became a manger of a copper mine north of Rehoboth.[115] By this means he financed his travelings all over the country. Elephant hunting, Andersson tried to go to Kunene once again, but not through Ovamboland. He tried through Kaokoveld, but he failed. He attempted to go to the east by way of Omandombe. This led Andersson to the "discovery" of the Okavango River in 1857. It was the same year that two Rhenish Missionary Society missionaries, C. H. Hahn and Johannes Rath, an English hunter, Frederick Joseph Green (1829–76), and a trader, Georg Bonfield (1836–61), visited Ovamboland as the second group of white people in that region since Galton and his companions six years earlier. Thomas Baines and James Chapman crossed Namibia from Botswana to Walvis Bay in 1861.

In 1864 hunters Frederick J. Green, W. C. Palgrave, J. Pereira, H. Smuts, R. Levis, and J. R. Todd visited Ovamboland. Green, Smuts and Pereira went on and reached the Kunene in the same year. While these three hunters proceeded to Kunene, Mrs. Green remained in Ovamboland with King Shikongo shaKalulu of the Ondonga tribe and gave birth on November 4, 1865 to Mary, the first white child to be born in Ovamboland.[116] The following year two hunters, C. T. Een and Axel W. Ericksson, also visited Ovamboland. Under the advice of Green, Andersson, who had become a rich merchant, built a small shop in Ondonga. This was run by Joseph Grendon, possibly at Omandongo. Grendon built Andersson a small apartment after Andersson sold his possessions at Otjimbingwe in 1864. Andersson and Eriksson attempted to reach Kunene, this time at last through Ovamboland, but on their way back to Ondonga both men died between Uukwambi and Uukwanyama.[117]

Although the white explorations of Namibia continued, those mentioned above were among the pioneers. Large numbers of white settlers were already noticeable in the early 1800s, especially under the auspices of the Christian Missionary Societies. James Frank Bassingthwaite[118] was the first permanent white settler in Namibia. When more Boer farmers were settling in about 1874, this kind of reaction was received from the Herero chiefs:

We have learnt with deep concern that a very extensive gathering of Dutch farmers has arrived . . . to settle. . . . They intend to make war on us and compel us to submit. . . . We have no unoccupied land for the admission of any other nation, more especially one who, we have been led to believe, has always looked upon the black tribes with scorn and indignation and who both recognize and practice slavery. . . . The Boers, like ourselves, have an irrevocable attachment for cattle. . . . They would require an extensive tract of country. . . .[119]

NOTES

1. Horst Drechsler, *"Let Us Die Fighting"*: *The Struggle of the Herero and Nama against German Imperialism (1884–1915)* (Zed Press, 1980), 17.

2. Eschel Rhoodie, *South West: The Last Frontier in Africa* (Johannesburg: Voortrekker Press, 1967), 1.

3. *This Is Namibia: A Pictorial Introduction* (London: International Defence and Aid Fund for Southern Africa, 1984), 6.

4. Shivute Usko Shivute, "20th Century Namibia. In Search of Independence: Changing International and Internal Strategies" (M.A. Thesis, University of Minnesota, 1985), 2. The richness of the country is one of the main reasons why South Africa remains recalcitrantly contumacious and refuses to give Namibia independence. If Namibia were a poor country, there would be no reason to pour millions of rand into the country for its "protection" without gaining anything from "protecting" it.

5. Theo-Ben Gurirab, "Statement on the Occasion of United Nations General Assembly Special Session on Namibia" (New York: UNO, 17 September 1986), 4–5.

6. Chief Hosea Kutako, 1947. See also *Church and Race in South Africa*, ed. David M. Paton (Naperville, Ill.: SCM Book Club, 1958), 125.

7. Thirteenth General Convention of the American Lutheran Church held 23–29 August 1986, Minneapolis, Minn., CC86.7.448.

8. *Namibia in the 1980s: A CIIR/BCC Position Paper* (London: Catholic Institute for International Relations and British Council of Churches, 1981), 7.

9. J. J. Kritzinger, *Sending en Kerk in Suidwes-Afrika*, Vol. 1 (Pretoria: Navorsingsverslag aan die Raad vir Geesteswetenskaplike Navorsing oor die kerkemaatskaplike situasie van die nie-blankes van Suidwes-Afrika, 1969), 1.

10. *Ibid.*, I.

11. Elizabeth S. Landis, *Namibian Liberation: Self-determination, Law and Politics* (New York: Churchmen for South Africa, 1982), 1.

12. *Namibia: Perspectives for National Reconstruction and Development* (Lusaka: United Nations Institute for Namibia, 1986), 28.

13. *Ibid.*, 21

14. *Ibid.*, 24–25.

15. J. M. Wallace-Hardrill, *The Barbarian West: The Early Middle Ages, A.D. 400–1000* (New York: Harper Torchbooks, 1962), 21.

16. Shivute Usko Shivute, "20th Century Namibia, In Search of Independence—Changing International and Internal Strategies" (M. A. Thesis, University of Minnesota, 1985), 102.

17. It was "considered disgrace for Christians (i.e., Europeans) to marry people of colour, even if they were free." Edward Roux, *Time Longer Than Rope: A History of the Black Man's Struggle for Freedom in South Africa* (Madison: The University of Wisconsin Press, 1964), 23.

18. Jan Knappert, *Namibia: Land and Peoples, Myths and Fables* (Leiden: E. J. Brill, 1981), 20.

19. Julius Baumann, *Van Sending tot Kerk, 1842–1967* (Karibib: Evangeliese Lutherse Kerk in S.W.A. (Rynse Sendingkerk, 1967)), 50.

20. Eschel Rhoodie, *South West: The Last Frontier in Africa* (Johannesburg: Voortrekker Press, 1967), 101.

21. Report of the Commission on Inquiry regarding the Cape Coloured Population in 1938, quoted by Alastair Matheson in "The Coloured People of the Cape" (London: Public Relations Office, South Africa House), 7–8. It also appears in Eugene P. Dvorin, *Racial Separation in South Africa* (University of Chicago Press, 1952), 61.

22. Roux, 23.
23. Knappert, 89.
24. Baumann, 44, 49.
25. *Ibid.*, 55.
26. Roland Oliver and Anthony Atmore, *Africa Since 1800* (London: Cambridge University Press, 1981), 57. Kaire Mbuende, *Namibia, the Broken Shield: Anatomy of Imperialism and Revolution* (Lund, 1986), 27–28.
27. Baumann, 134.
28. Ruth First, *South West Africa* (Maryland: Penguin Books, 1963), 35.
29. J. Du Plessis, *A History of Christian Missions in South Africa* (Cape Town: C. Struik, 1965), 207.
30. Rhoodie, 114.
31. *Encyclopedia Britannica* (New York, 1974), 9:585.
32. Knappert, 71.
33. First, 37.
34. Knappert, 72.
35. Erkki Laurmaa, *Afrika jUuningininomutenja* (Helsinki: Finse Sending, 1949), 12.
36. *Encyclopedia Britannica*, 9:585.
37. Knappert, 72.
38. Note that the Ovaherero (Herero) is also a tribe within the Ovaherero (Herero) nation.
39. *South Africa '78: Official Year Book* (South Africa, 1978), 107.
40. The other two were Ovakavango and Ovambo.
41. Rhoodie, 118–19.
42. H. Vedder, *South West Africa in Early Times* (Oxford University Press, 1938), 131–53.
43. Laurmaa, 12–13. *Note*: In today's Oshiwambo language, j = y, except in "ndj" combination; u = u or w; "Oshauana" (Oshawana) = Botswana; and "Aashauana" (Aashawana) means people of Botswana; c = th ("c" is not present in the Oshiwambo alphabet; however, it begins to appear today through foreign names and terminologies); d = dh; Ngamitale = Lake Ngami; Afrika jUuningininomutenja = Namibia (South West Africa).
44. Richard Gray, "Southern Africa and Madagascar" in *The Cambridge History of Africa: 1600–1700*, Vol. 4 (London: 1975), 422.
45. John H. Wellington, *South West Africa and its Human Issues* (Oxford Clarendon Press, 1967), 145.
46. Sir James George, *Anthologia Anthropologia: The Native Races of Africa and Madagascar* (London: Percy Lund Humphries & Co., Ltd., 1938), 105.
47. Shivute, 6.
48. Mburumba Kerina, *Namibia: The Making of a Nation* (New York: Books in Focus, 1981), 47.
49. *Ibid.*, 5. Cites the *Encyclopedia of Southern Africa* (New York, 1961), 224.
50. Michael Scott, *A Time to Speak* (New York: Doubleday and Company, Inc., 1958), 96.
51. Gerhard Tötemeyer, *Namibia: Old and New, Traditional and Modern Leaders in Ovamboland* (London: C. Hurst and Co., 1978), 3.
52. Oliver and Atmore, 103.
53. According to F. P. Noble, *The Redemption of Africa*, Vol. 1 (New York: Fleming H. Revell Co., 1893), 301: "Namaqua or Nama = Kwa is the old spelling. = Kwa

(=qua) means people and is superfluous. So with=ra in Damara." See also note 46 below in Vigne, 7.

54. Knappert, 86.

55. *Ibid.*, 88–89. *To Be Born a Nation: The Liberation Struggle for Namibia* (London: Zed Press, 1981), 10. *Standard Encyclopedia of Southern Africa*, Vol. 10 (SLE-TUN, Nasau Limited, 1974), 157–58. Five Nama tribes which came from the Cape were: //Ai-xa//Ain of Afrikaner; Gei-/Khauan of Amraal in Gobabis; !Kowesin of Witbooi in Gibeon; /Hei-/Khauan in Berseba; and !Aman in Bethanie.

56. First, 32. "The Nama came at some ancient time, perhaps from north-eastern Africa, perhaps from an even further place of origin." Randolph Vigne, *A Dwelling Place of Our Own: The Story of the Namibian Nation* (London: IDAF, 1975), 7.

57. First, 32. Also see Rhoodie, 121. While both agree on the term's origin, First seems to be more certain of the meaning than Rhoodie, who says: "The origin of the word Orlam is uncertain but it may have been a perversion of the Malay "Orang Lama", meaning *old* (and hence wise) man." According to H. Vedder in his *South West Africa in Early Times*, 171:

> "Orlam is a word of Malay origin, derived from the Malay 'Orang lama', an old person, and came to mean 'one who has been a long time in the land', thus 'one who knows the world thoroughly', and so 'one who is wide awake'. . . . The [Nama] tribe of Orlams adopted this name because they had a great opinion of their own abilities. Amraal is [also] a contraction of Admiral."

58. Laurmaa, 11.

59. John O. Choules and Thomas Smith, eds., *The Origin of Missions*, Vol. 2 (Boston: Gould, Kendall and Lincoln, 1837), 138–40. Se also Du Plessis, 115. Speaking of the Nama, Albrecht says in 1806:

> "The whole nation is divided into different tribes, each of them distinguished by a particular name and governed by a chief. Their usual food is milk and meat; but some of them, who are so poor as to have no cattle at all, are obliged to live on the gum which they gather from the kameeldoorn (a mimosa), and on bulbs, roots and wild honey. They hunt the smaller species of buck, and kill them with arrows or assegais; but the larger game they sometimes catch in holes, which they dig near the wells of fresh water. For clothing they make use of *karosses*, made of sheepskins. In summer these are thrown aside and the men go quite naked, except for a small piece of jackal's skin. The women are clothed with *karosses* like the men; but also throw them off in summer, and wear only a small apron of skin. Their social pleasure consists almost exclusively in dancing. Only the men are performers at the dancing party, and the exercise consists chiefly in jumping and violently shaking the body to the time of music made by whistles, which are cut out of reeds. The men employ themselves in caring for the cattle and in hunting; the women in milking the cattle." (Du Plessis)

60. It is difficult to determine whether the correct plural term is *Ovambos* or *Ovambo*. In the Oshiwambo languages the singular form is *omuwambo*, whereas the plural form is *aawambo* or *ovawambo*. *Ovambos* can be translated as *Ovawambo* instead of *Ovavambo*. The difficulty is caused by the fact that the original term is not known. It might have been *ambo* as a singular form, or it might have always been *ovambo* in a plural form. In that case, to be translated as *Ovambos* would mean *Aawambo* or *Ovawambo* in the Oshiwambo language. Possibilities of the term's origin might be: *ovo mbo* meaning "there they are," *ovaampo* meaning "they belong there," or *ovawa mbo* meaning "those (people) are nice (good)." If this is acceptable, then the singular will be difficult to find, because *Ovambo* would be a pronoun, not a noun.

61. For the Ovambo belief in Kalunga, read Teddy Aarni, *The Kalunga Concept in Ovambo Religion from 1870 Onwards* (Stockholm: Almqvist & Wicksell International, 1982).

62. Tötemeyer, 3.

63. To Anglicize the terms leave out the prefix "oshi-", for example, "Oshikwa-nyama" becomes "Kwanyama," etc.

64. I have studied several languages, including Latin, Spanish, English, Dutch, Afrikaans, German, Hebrew, Greek and many African languages (the Oshiwambo languages, among others). Therefore, this relation is done by experience of study rather than by any scientific means of linguistic analysis. Linguistically the relation may be different.

65. Barbara Tyrrell, *The Tribal People of Southern Africa* (T. V. Bulpin, 1976), 6.

66. Vedder, 15.

67. First, 98.

68. Richard Gibson, *African Liberation Movements: Contemporary Struggles Against White Minority Rule* (New York: Oxford University Press, 1972), 117.

69. Tötemeyer, 45.

70. *South Africa 1975*, p. 107; and *South Africa 1978*, p. 97 (Year Books).

71. C. G. Seligman, *Races of Africa* (New York: Henry Holt & Co., 1930), 25–26. The San's "facial type and skin colour suggest a people of Oriental ancestry and it is said that at birth the babies show what is known as the Mongolian spot which disappears in early infancy. However, these are matters of conjecture and controversy." See Tyrrell, 6.

72. *Ibid.*, 27.

73. Wellington, 133. Baboons are also used as water reconnaisances. They are trapped during severe drought when water is very scarce. They are fed with food which makes them thirsty, then released. After being released and being very thirsty, the baboon runs straight to the nearest available water while the people follow behind. In this way people would discover where water was available.

74. *South Africa 1975*, p. 107.

75. Wellington, 135.

76. *South Africa 1975*, p. 108.

77. Peter Carstens, *Academic American Encyclopedia*, 17, 49–50.

78. Stanley Schoeman and Elna Schoeman, *Namibia: World Bibliographical Series*, Vol. 53 (Clio Press, 1984), 46.230. The first white person to settle permanently in Namibia was an Englishman, James Frank Bassingthwaite, who left England in 1842. By white settlers we mean people of European ancestry who migrated to South Africa and Namibia. They have not only settled but have appropriated land and dominated the politics of the country by racist policies and delayed and denied independence to Namibia.

79. David B. Barrett, *Schism and Renewal in Africa* (Nairobi: Oxford University Press, 1968), 125.

80. See these statistics in the United Nations Council for Namibia in the Namibia teaching aid material of July 1984.

81. Rhoodie, 102.

82. V. M. Hillyer and E. G. Huey, *The Modern World* (New York: Meredith Press, 1966), 16.

83. J. H. Parry, *The Establishment of the European Hegemony: 1415–1715* (New York: Harper Torchbooks, 1961), 29.

84. *Ibid.*, 33.

85. James Duffy, *Portuguese Africa* (Massachusetts: Harvard University Press, 1959), 6.

86. W. J. De Kock, ed., *Dictionary of South Africa Biography*, Vol. 1 (Cape Town: Nasionale Boekhandel, BPK, 1968), 153.

87. Some sources mention either 1485 or 1486, but 1484 seems to be more convincing as it appears in more and older sources, plus the evidence of the inscription found at Cape Cross.

88. This was formerly thought to be the island of San Salvador, but in 1986 it was said that the actual island was another island about 61 miles south of San Salvador in the Bahamas. This argument appeared on a television program.

89. Rhoodie, 103.

90. *Ibid.* "Chips were recovered from the original mound in 1953, and are today in the Windhoek museum." De Kock, 154. Compare also the inscription in Oshiwambo: "Okuza keshito lyuuyuni sho kwa piti omimvo 6684, no kokuvalwa kwaKristus 1484, emwene omunene Don Joao gwaPortugal okwa lombwele Diego Cao, omukwiita ofule a dhike emanya ndika." Laurmaa, 30–31.

91. Duffy, 104.

92. P. J. M. McEwan, *Africa from Early Times to 1800* (London: Oxford University Press, 1968), 216.

93. De Kock, 154.

94. The dates of Diaz are very inconsistent in the sources; it is, however between 1486 and 1488.

95. De Kock, 244.

96. Parry, 38.

97. De Kock, 210. "In India [Da Gama] bombarded Calicut, and in the name of Christianity was guilty of many actions which today would be branded as atrocities." (p. 200)
"The third Indies fleet, commanded again by Vasco da Gama, sailed in 1502. This was a powerful and well-armed force, fourteen sails in all, and with it da Gama carried out a heavy bombardment of the town of Calicut, an important event in the history of naval gunnery as well as in that of Indo-European relations. Da Gama also fought and won the first naval pitched battle in the struggle for control in the East, against a fleet equipped by the Malabar Arabs. The Arab fleet . . . was almost annihilated . . . by Parry." (p. 39)
This shows the European spirit of exterminating others in the pursuit of new lands wherever they went.

98. De Kock, 200.

99. McEwan, 199.

100. Frank J. Parker, *South Africa: Lost Opportunities* (Toronto: Lexington Books, 1983), 88; and Larumaa, 33.

101. Oliver and Atmore, 164. "It was not until the middle of the nineteenth century that Cape traders from Walvis Bay and Portuguese from Mocamedes penetrated northern Namibia and southern Angola, and traded fire arms to the chiefdoms, which led, fairly rapidly, to their breakdown."

102. First, 62.

103. Gray, 439.

104. *Ibid.*, 440.

105. *Ibid.*, 445.

106. Knappert, 14.

107. *To Be Born a Nation*, 151.

108. D. W. Kruger, ed., *Dictionary of South Africa Biography*, Vol. 2 (Johannesburg: Tafelberg-Uitgewers, Ltd., 1972), 134.

109. *Ibid.*, 135.

110. "Damaraland" and "Hereroland" were used interchangeably. Herero were often referred to as Damara. "The Herero used to be called Cattle-Damara. . . . The Dama themselves used to be distinguished by the epithet 'Mountain' Dama, in German *Die Bergdama*. . . ." Knappert, 72. The Herero were "misnamed the Damara by a confusion of the Nama word for them". First, 28.

111. "Chikorongo-onkompe" does not sound Oshindonga or Oshiwambo. I think the proper sound or name is probably Shikolongombe" or "Shikongo shaAngombe". See Eric Axelson, *South African Explorers* (Oxford University press, 1954), 285.

112. See note 110 above.

113. Axelson, 291.

114. *Ibid.*, 299–300.

115. *Ibid.*, 306.

116. Toivo E. Tirronen, *Nakambalekanene* (Oniipa: Oshinyanyangidho shaELOK, 1977), 11.

117. *Ibid.*, 11–12.

118. Colin E. Bell, "South Africa" in *Namibia*, eds. Schoeman and Schoeman, 46.

119. First, 67.

How the Church came to Namibia

II

HISTORY HAS WITNESSED the heroism of Christian men and women who have obeyed the commission of Jesus Christ by leaving their homes, families, communities and countries to go to "unknown" lands and peoples preaching the Good News of human brotherhood and everlasting life in God. Those who lived by the gospel touched the hearts of their hearers and transformed their lives in many ways. In most cases this was done or happened through much hardship and unceasing patience nourished by burning Christian love within the breasts of preachers and missionaries.

Although mission work can be traced back to the Apostles, especially Paul, there was a time when the church did not embark on mission or what is known now as foreign mission. G. P. Fisher, quoted by Theodore Huggenvik, puts it this way:

More than a hundred years before the beginning of the Reformation, the missionary activity of the church was suspended. If much had already been accomplished in the spread of the Gospel, quite as much still remained to be done.[1]

The Roman Catholic Church took the lead in reviving missionary activity. The Jesuits (the Society of Jesus), one of the major forces in the Counter-Reformation, was organized in 1539 with the idea of foreign missions. Again, to quote Theodore Huggenvik:

The Jesuits had foreign missions on the program from the beginning of their organization, and in 1622 was organized the congregation for the Propaganda of the Faith in Rome. This congregation directs the missionary activity of the Catholic Church, both among heathens and Protestants.[2]

The Protestants' foreign missionary activity was begun by the founding of the Society for the Propagation of the Gospel in England in 1701. The founding of other Protestant missionary societies followed. Except in Ethiopia, what Christianity had existed in Africa had been replaced by the Islamic faith. Islam came to Africa in the seventh century and covered most of North Africa. Though Spanish Franciscans had been working as "missionaries" in the Canary Islands off the northwest coast of Africa since 1402,[3] it was the Jesuits who, working first in Ethiopia in 1557, went to do mission work in

Africa for the first time since the collapse of Christianity in Africa during the seventh century.[4]

The first Christians in southern Africa were not a direct result of mission work in the region. Those Christians did not come with a planned operation for missions when they left Europe. There was no overall grand design for evangelism. The idea of evangelizing the indigenous people of southern Africa developed only after the European discovery of a trading route from Europe to the East via South Africa and the establishment of Portuguese colonial settlements along the coast of Africa.

Another factor which brought the advance of the Church in the region was the Dutch settlement at the Cape of Good Hope in 1652. Colonial development and the reinforcement of the European troops in southern Africa to conduct war against indigenous resistance always brought new Christians. These were soldiers, colonists, traders, explorers, officials and persecuted Christians such as the Huguenots. The French Protestants, or Huguenots, as they were called after 1557, came to South Africa as refugees in 1688. They came with their own pastor and settled at Stellenbosch and Paarl (Drakenstein).

As these Christians organized their own congregations, pastors were drawn to this part of Africa. Even though there was no organized mission, three native women were baptized, including Eva, who was a servant to Jan van Riebeeck's family and who served as an interpreter. The date of the baptism was May 3, 1662. The other two women baptized with Eva were Sara and Cornelia. Eventually, Eva got married in the church to a Danish man who worked with the Dutch East India Company. Sara is reported to have committed suicide in 1671 after she had been deceived by a European gentleman who had promised to marry her. Cornelia was never married.[5]

The first missionary proper to South Africa was a Moravian, George Schmidt, in 1737. Schmidt was a devout member of the Moravian Brethren called *Unitas Fratrum*. At one time Schmidt had been a prisoner for six years in Austria. Schmidt stayed six years in South Africa and returned to Europe.

The second group of missionaries to South Africa arrived in 1799. They were under the leadership of a Dutchman, Van der Kemp, and under the auspices of the London Missionary Society.

Without going into detail, it is worth noting that political development in South Africa also affected mission work in the region. Missionary activities changed from time to time depending on the nature and background of the government in charge of South Africa. There have been at least six different administrative periods in the history of colonial South Africa. These periods could be individually examined, but for the purposes of this study we will only mention them in summary:

1. 1652–1795 South Africa under Holland
2. 1795–1802 South Africa under Britain
3. 1802–1806 South Africa under Holland
4. 1806–1910 South Africa under Britain
5. 1910–1961 The Union of South Africa under the white population
6. 1961–1986 The white minority Republic of South Africa.

The importance of noting these periods of political change lies in the fact that conflicts between church and state in the region need to be assessed in terms of the political dynamics of each specific period.

PIONEER MISSIONS

The London Missionary Society (LMS)

The very first missionaries to come to Namibia belonged to the London Missionary Society. This missionary society was established in London in September 1795. This was the same year Britain took control of the Cape Colony from Holland for the first time. It was known as "The Missionary Society" until 1818, when it came to be known as "The London Missionary Society." The organization of the Society was the immediate result of William Carey's Bengal Mission in India. Carey was a missionary of the Baptist Missionary Society who, through his correspondence with friends in Europe, made the appeal to Evangelicals other than Baptists to undertake their own missions overseas. Similar societies, the Edinburgh and Glasgow Missionary Societies, were founded through the same appeal in 1796, and the Netherlands Missionary Society in 1797. Other European Missionary Societies followed.

The London Society (LMS) began as an interdenominational organization including Episcopalians, Methodists, Presbyterians, and Independents or Congregationalists. However, in due course the Episcopalians, Methodists and Presbyterians formed their own missionary societies. The main supporter of the London Missionary Society was then the Congregationalist Churches of England, but the Society's fundamental principle remained the same:

That its design is not to send Presbyterianism, Independency, Episcopacy, or any other form of church order and government (about which there may be difference of opinion among serious persons), but the glorious gospel of the blessed God, to the heathen, and that it shall be left (as it ought to be left) to the minds of the persons whom God may call into the fellowship of His Son from among them, to assume for themselves such form of church government as to them shall appear most agreeable to the Word of God.[6]

The sole object of the London Missionary Society was the spreading of the knowledge of Christ among the "heathen and other unenlightened nations." On March 31, 1799, four London Missionary Society missionaries arrived in South Africa. They were J. J. Kicherer, Dr. Johannes Theodorus Van der Kemp, John Edmonds and William Edwards. By that time only the Moravian Brethren of Germany were missionaries in South Africa, their mission having grown from the work of George Schmidt. Schmidt came to South Africa in 1737 and left that country by the 1740s. It was from South Africa that the work of the LMS was extended to Namibia a few years later.

In 1805 (or January 1806) new recruits from Holland came to South Africa under the auspices of the London Missionary Society. They included the two brothers, Christian and Abraham Albrecht, and J. Seidenfaden. These men were sent for the purpose of going to Namibia. On their way there, they set up temporary stations at "Stille Hoop" (Silent Hope) and "Blyde Uitkomst" (Happy Deliverance or Happy Results). These stations are in South Africa, south of the Orange River. When they crossed the river, they went to the place which they called "Blydeverwagting," where Chief Jager Afrikaner of the Orlams (Nama) had lived with his people since 1793. From Chief Afrikaner the missionaries moved northward to Warmbad and worked among the Bondelswarts (Nama).

In 1811 the Warmbad mission station was unexpectedly destroyed by the Namibians under the leadership of Chief Jager Afrikaner. At the time of the mission's destruction, the missionaries were on a journey to Cape Town because of Abraham Albrecht's health. Abraham died before they reached Cape Town, at Bothma's farm, Heuningberg, near Portville. Receiving news of the plunder while he was in the Cape, Christian was in despair and wanted to go back to Germany. Christian and other missionaries decided to remain at Pella (named after Pella in Palestine, where Christians took refuge during the period of the siege of Jerusalem by Titus in 70 A.D.), south of the Orange River. About five hundred Namibian Christians from Warmbad followed the missionaries to Pella.

The furthering of mission work in Namibia after the destruction of Warmbad was a challenge to new missionaries to go there. These new missions took two directions: one to "Blydeverwagting" and the other to "Bethanie." We shall examine each one.

SECOND MISSION TO "BLYDEVERWAGTING"

"Blydeverwagting" was the first place in Namibia where the Albrecht brothers set up their first station before they moved to Warmbad. Through these brothers, Chief Afrikaner came to be interested in the missionaries' work. After the destruction of Warmbad, there was no longer any mission in Namibia. However, Afrikaner wanted his people to be taught by the missionaries. He corresponded with John Campbell in South Africa, asking for missionaries. Campbell was then Superintendent of the London Missionary Society in the Cape Colony and was in a position to commission a missionary and send him to a specific place.

In the meantime, five missionaries from Germany came to South Africa under the protection of the LMS. They were J. L. H. Ebner, Schmelen, Sass, Helm, and Messer. They arrived in the Cape Colony on September 13, 1811. In 1815 Campbell commissioned Ebner, who by then was working at Pella, to go to Namibia. Chief Afrikaner's request was, therefore, met.

Ebner resided at Chief Jager Afrikaner's residence. Soon other missionaries received the good news that the chief and many of his people, including two of his sons, David and Jacobus, and his brother, were baptized by Ebner on July 23, 1816. The chief took the name Christian as his baptismal name. Although Ebner was in South Africa the following year, he returned to Namibia to resume his work on January 26, 1818.

It was in 1818 that Robert Moffat (1795–1883) arrived at Chief Afrikaner's palace. At this time "Blydeverwagting" was renamed "Vrede Berg" (Peace Mountain) by Ebner; it was later changed to "Jerusalem." Moffat was well received despite his fear of what Ebner told him back at the Cape, i.e., that these people were "wicked, suspicious, and dangerous people, baptized as well as unbaptized."[7] Ebner never trusted the Namas, although they never did any harm to him. Two months after Moffat's arrival, Ebner left the mission in bitter and violent dispute with the Afrikaners and subsequently returned to Germany. Ebner was known as a man of little patience and tact. He quarreled often with the Africans. His departure was a direct result of his behavior.

Moffat remained at "Blydeverwagting." He worked there and also around Warmbad. Being at Afrikaner's residence, Moffat gained the confidence of the people. Mention has already been made that Afrikaner was an outlawed[8] person with one thousand pounds offered on his head. Moffat managed to reconcile Afrikaner with the Cape Governor, Lord Charles Somerset. To finalize this reconciliation process, Moffat took the chief to Cape Town in 1819. "The very Governor who had at first refused Moffat permission to proceed was now so impressed that he showed his goodwill by a present to Afrikaner of an excellent waggon, valued at eighty pounds sterling."[9] After this journey to Cape Town, Moffat never went back to Namibia. Instead he went to New Lattakoo in Botswana, where he arrived the following year. The mission was left without a missionary.

SCHMELEN IN BETHANIE

The second direction was taken by Johann Heinrich Schmelen in 1814. Schmelen was invited by the Nama of Bethanie to come and establish a mission station. At that time Schmelen was working at Pella together with other missionaries. In 1814 Schmelen decided to go to Namibia and established a mission station there the following year. His experiences at Bethanie drove him to write: "Dass ein Volk glaubig werden soll auf einen Tag."[10]

From Bethanie, Schmelen

decided to move yet further north and once again the ox, "Koeskobus", was saddled. His blankets made of skins, which also served as a saddle, and his Bible were all the luggage he had. During a period of seven years he lived off the land, eating the same food as the [indigenous] people among whom he laboured and he wore clothing made of skins and hides as they did. He suffered many tribulations, but he steadfastly practised his vocation.[11]

In 1818 Schmelen went back to South Africa. A year later he was able to come back to Namibia and found that his former labor had vanished. He had to start again. Drought and a locust plague struck the country. This forced Schmelen to move back south of the Orange River with some of his followers in 1824. The drought threatened Namibia for four years. After this, Schmelen came back to his lonely mission field.

Apart from preaching, teaching and writing, Schmelen also visited Windhoek (1823), Walvis Bay (1824) and Okahandja (1830). His refuge in South Africa during the time of drought in Namibia gave him a chance to arrange possibilities for the printing of his Nama version of the Gospels, which he translated with the help of his Nama wife. The printing was done in 1831. In 1829 Schmelen established another mission station at Komaggas, where he stayed for the rest of his life.

Since Schmelen was getting old, in 1838 he requested help from the London Missionary Society so that the Society would continue his work in Namibia. However, during the 1840s the LMS decided to transfer its mission stations in the area to the Rhenish Missionary Society. The Rev. F. H. Kleinschmidt, Schmelen's son-in-law, married to Johanna (Hanna) from Schmelen's first marriage, was sent to assist the old man. Kleinschmidt (of the Rhenish Mission) arrived at Komaggas on June 17, 1840. Schmelen and Kleinschmidt stayed together at Komaggas. These were the last days of the London Missionary Society in Namibia. On July 26, 1848 the hardworking missionary and dedicated servant J. H. Schmelen died at Komaggas at the age of 71. We shall hear more later about Kleinschmidt in connection with the Rhenish Mission.

THE ENGLISH WESLEYAN METHODIST MISSIONARY SOCIETY

The Wesleyan Missionary Society was organized in Leeds on October 6, 1813. The rules and constitution were finalized in 1818. Wesleyan Methodists are known for being "strictly missionary"[12] in character. From its early stages this society extended its mission beyond Britain and Ireland to India, America, Sri Lanka, the South Seas, Mauritius, the Mediterranean and southern and western Africa.

The Society has diverse theological roots, including Wycliffe, John Huss, Zinzendorf, Francke, Whitefield, the Wesley brothers (John and Charles) and finally Dr. Thomas Coke of Oxford University, who associated himself with the Wesleys and is the first well-known foreign missionary of Wesleyan Methodism. In 1786 Coke was sent to Nova Scotia, Canada, but he ended up in the West Indies, in Antigua, and also eventually in Ceylon (Sri Lanka) in 1813.

About 1806 British soldiers in Cape Town, South Africa, organized the first Methodist meetings. By 1812 these soldiers requested the Wesleyan Missionary Society in England to send a pastor to South Africa. This pastor would serve the soldiers and develop mission work. As a result, the Rev. John McKenny was sent to Cape Town in 1813, but the Governor, Lord Somerset, refused him permission to hold worship services. J. Du Plessis contends that:

Lord Charles Somerset's reasons for withholding from McKenny the right to preach were apparently these, [sic]—that the duly appointed chaplains of the

Church of England would resent his labouring among the soldiers, and that the ministers of the Dutch Reformed Church would take his work on behalf of the slaves with an equally ill grace.[13]

This prohibition from preaching forced McKenny to decide to go on to Sri Lanka. The Methodist soldiers persisted in their appeal. Another Wesleyan minister, Barnabas Shaw, and his wife were sent to South Africa in 1816. He, too, was refused permission to preach. Shaw took things into his own hands and began to preach to the indigenous people without permission. He regarded himself as a "missionary to the heathen." Two years after Shaw's arrival in the Cape, as he was about to seek a mission station site, Schmelen of the London Missionary Society visited the Cape colony. By that time Schmelen had been working in Namibia for four years, since 1814. Schmelen convinced Shaw that a ripe field for mission existed in Namaland.

The two men, Schmelen and Shaw, travelled together to the north. On the way they were met by a Nama chief who was going to the Cape seeking a teacher for his people. Shaw seized this opportunity and eventually built a mission station at Leliefontein on the Kamiesberg south of the Orange River. While working on the Kamiesberg range (from 1820), Shaw made several journeys to Namibia with a view to establish a permanent Wesleyan mission in that territory.

In 1825 three Wesleyan preachers, William Threlfall and two Namas (Jacobus Links and Johannes Jager), left Leliefontein for Warmbad in Namibia. All three men were murdered by the Namibians just north of Warmbad. Very often, whites and missionaries ignored advice from blacks or "pagans" respectively, thinking too much of themselves despite their lack of experience and knowledge of contextual diplomacy. Threlfall fell into this error. The advice was given him, based on the knowledge of customary rules and regulations, that it was a risky business to enter other people's lands without their consent. Even though there were no passports, there were codes to be followed.

When he [Threlfall] arrived at Kammanoup, in Great Namaqualand, the chief strongly advised him to return; but he [was] determined upon going forward, and prosecuting his intended journey. . . . A few days after they left Kammanoup, they arrived at a Bushmen [San] kraal, where . . . [they] were murdered. . . .[14]

However, having been advised, Threlfall made sure that the chief would not be held responsible for anything which might happen to the three preachers on their journey to the north. Therefore, the following letter was written before the journey, which was intended to "discover" Damaraland, was taken.

Warm Bath, July 19th, 1825

To Whom It May Concern:

We, William Threlfall, Jacob Links and Johannes Jagger, do, by this writing, make it known, that, if we never return from the Fish River, or the nations and tribes to the north of it, that no unpleasant reflections ought to be cast on the captain and tribe called Bondle Zwaarts, because they have permitted us to pass through their country, into the dangers before us; from which, they say, we shall never escape with our lives. They have faithfully warned us; but being disposed to proceed, in what we all think our duty to God and fellow men, should we never return, we acquit them from all guilt in our misfortune.
    William Threlfall
    Jacob Links
His X marks: Joannes Jagger[15]

Although it can be seen as stupidity to ignore the strong warnings about danger, one is nevertheless fascinated by the strong willpower and commitment of the three preachers. Of course, sometimes people succeeded despite such dangers. This incident remains both a lesson and a warning from history.

For the time being, any attempt to establish a Wesleyan Methodist mission station in Namibia was halted. However, pleas from the Namibian chiefs for teachers were ceaseless. With some degree of success, another attempt was made in 1832 at Warmbad, but it was not until 1834 that a permanent station was founded there by Edward Cook. In 1840 Rev. Joseph Tindall arrived to assist Rev. Cook. Unfortunately, Rev. Cook died three years later. Rev. Ridsdale came to Warmbad in 1844, and Rev. John Bailie joined the staff four years later when Ridsdale was appointed pastor at Wynberg in the Cape.

Other stations followed at Nossob District—Leonardville and Gobabis under Tindall from 1842 to 1850 among the people of Amraal Lamberts, and at Windhoek under Haddy from 1844 to 1850 among the Afrikaners' tribe. Other stations were formed, viz., Concordville, Elephant Fountain, and Wesley Vale. Various difficulties, including lack of supplies and encounters with nomadic people searching for grazing land, plagued the Wesleyan mission work. The Society was no longer able to send in new missionaries. Therefore, in 1867 the Wesleyan Society requested that the Rhenish Mission take over their work.

THE LUTHERANS

Sixty per cent of Namibian Christians today are Lutherans. These Lutherans are for the most part credited to the German and Finnish Lutheran missionaries who courageously worked in Namibia beginning in the mid-1800s. However, the Lutherans did not find Namibia a completely unchristian country. The missionaries of the London Missionary Society and the Wesleyan Missionary Society had worked there since 1805. Nevertheless, the Lutherans were the first to establish mission stations throughout the territory from Warmbad to Engela and from Gobabis to Swakopmund. It was these stations which later became independent churches under the leadership of the Namibians themselves. The Lutheran influence was so strong that it never occurred to most people that there were other missionaries before the Lutherans, as indeed there had been for at least thirty-seven years!

THE RHENISH MISSIONARY SOCIETY (RMS)

By the eighth century (May 777) Germany was converted to Christianity by the method of death by sword or baptism. The conversion of the Saxons was entwined with Prince Charlemagne's imperialism. In 782 he "promulgated the capitulary of Saxony which made it a crime punishable by death not to accept Christian baptism or to show disrespect to Christianity by not fasting during sacred seasons."[16] The method was cruel and must be considered unchrisitan, but it was from such a background of Christian missions to Germany that the Reformation of Martin Luther was later to be born. It was from this background that missionaries to foreign countries came. No one will endorse the method, but, again, Germany did become a Christian country by this method.

In 1799, over a thousand years after Germany was converted to Christianity, various parts of Germany experienced an awakening spirit for missions by the success of the London Missionary Society. In fact, this was the' year when twelve pious laymen at Elberfeld formed a little prayer group or circle of mission friends (*ookuume ketumo*) which became the root out of which the RMS later evolved. The society at Elberfeld inaugurated the Bergische Bible and Wupperthal Tract Societies. It published a paper called "Reports of the Extension of the Kingdom of Jesus, Especially among the Heathen" ("*Nachrichten von der Ausbreitung des Reiches Jesu, insbesondere unter den Heiden*"). It also contributed to the seminary at Berlin, Halle Institution, and the Moravian Society.

The Barmen Society was founded in 1815 and contributed financially to kindred societies; it also established a seminary at Barmen. The two societies, the Elberfeld and the Barmen, formed a union and developed the direction of the foreign mission concerns.

In 1828 delegates from these societies—Elberfeld, Barmen, Cologne, and Wesel—met at Mettmann. They agreed to form the "United Rhenish Missionary Society" ("*Vereinigte Rheinische Missions-Gesellschaft*"), committed to "the training and sending forth of Christian missionaries to non-Christian nations."[17] The society was confirmed by Friedrich Wilhelm II on July 24, 1829. The center of the Rhenish Mission was at Barmen. At that time Barmen was on the borders of the Rhine and was situated in the kingdom of Würtemburg, which later became a constituent part of Prussia. Three-fourths of its contributions came from the provinces of Rhineland and Westphalia.

The Rhenish Mission Society (RMS) was formed out of the Lutheran and Reformed traditions. There are historical arguments about how Lutheran the RMS was. "The first German society to work in South Africa was the Rhenish which, like the Basel Society, is not wholly Lutheran,"[18] asserts one historian. But another witness makes this assessment: "The Rhenish missionaries pledged strict adherence to Lutheran doctrine and principles."[19] In fact: "In 1817 to observe the 300th anniversary of the Reformation, King Frederick William III of Prussia caused Lutherans and Reformed churches in Prussia to be combined into one Evangelical [Protestant] Church."[20] Individual congregations were allowed to remain either Lutheran or Reformed.

In 1829 the first four missionaries of the RMS arrived in Cape Town, South Africa, under the charge of Dr. Philip of the London Missionary Society. They were T. von Wurmb, J. C. Leopoldt, G. A. Zahn and P. D. Lückhoff. Two of them ministered to the slaves, Lückhoff in Stellenbosch and Zahn in Tulbagh. The other two went towards the north among the Nama and established Wupperthal in the District of Clanwilliam in 1830 and Ebenhaeser station in 1832.

When these missionaries arrived, the Cape white settlement was 177 years old, established in 1652. Before their arrival, mission work was already established in the Cape and in the Eastern Province by various mission societies. They were the London Missionary Society and the Wesleyan, Scottish, Moravian and Zuid Afrikaanse Mission Societies. The LMS and the Wesleyans were also working in both Little and Great Namaland.

In 1840 the work of the LMS in Namaland was transferred to the RMS. LMS work had been commenced there in 1805 by the Albrecht brothers. Their mission station at Warmbad had been destroyed in 1811 by Jager Afrikaner in retaliation against Hans Dreyer's relatives.

During the earlier years of the Namaqua mission, Jager Afrikaner had borne himself somewhat quietly, and had refrained from raiding the colonial border. In 1811, however, he was provoked by an act of deceit perpetrated upon him by one Hans Dreyer, a Hottentot, whom in retaliation he killed; and not content with that, he attacked and robbed Seidenfaden's station at the Kamiesbergen at which Hans resided. A feud was thus engendered between the relatives of the murdered Hans and Jager. The former called to their assistance the Namaquas of Warm Bath. The missionaries were away at Cape Town; the community at Warm Bath . . . decided to cast in their lot with the Kamiesbergen people, and to defy Jager. . . . This so enraged the freebooter that he launched his force . . . defeated them, and reduced the mission station to a heap of ashes.[21]

After the Warmbad destruction, some of its residents fled to Pella, south of the Orange River, where Albrecht was working. Schmelen, another LMS missionary, established Bethanie mission station in 1814, where he labored until 1824. Many people became Christians through his preaching and service.

Although the LMS relinquished its mission stations in Namaland to the RMS, the Wesleyans continued to hold possession of Warmbad (Warm Bath or Nisbeth Bath). But the time came when the Wesleyans were no longer able to send new missionaries to Namibia (Namaland). That led the RMS to take the opportunity to obtain full entrance into Warmbad and to monopolize the mission work in Namibia, at least in the southern and central parts of the country.

In 1842 an artist and missionary of the RMS, Hans Christian Knudson, a Norwegian by birth, came to Bethanie—Schmelen's former station. This mission station was among the Orlams (Nama) tribe, descendants of the Cape Colony Nama who had lost their original language and spoke Afrikaans ("broken Dutch")[22] instead. Chief David Christian was their leader. When Knudson arrived, these people rejoiced at having their own missionary again, since Schmelen had left eighteen years earlier. Severe droughts soon struck the area, making difficult preaching and catechizing. People were scattered in the search for resources of survival. Another painful event which occurred at that time was the arrival of a trader who brought along brandy and firearms to Bethanie.

Between 1847 and 1849 Knudson was in Europe while the Rev. Samuel Hahn took care of Bethanie mission station. When Knudson returned, Hahn trekked to Berseba. Hahn and his African assistant, Christian Tibot, got good results among the people of Paul Goliath at Berseba, where they had recently trekked. Berseba had good water and pasture; therefore, this trek of Goliath's people provoked Oasib, Chief of the Rooi Nasie (Red Nation, another Nama tribe). But through these two missionaries peace was restored between the two tribes.

Heinrich Kleinschmidt (Schmelen's son-in-law) and his catechist, Jan Bam, visited Bethanie and proceeded to Windhoek in 1842. However, a Wesleyan missionary from Warmbad had baptized about twenty people in Windhoek shortly before their arrival. Kleinschmidt told Jonker Afrikaner that he could not do mission work among Jonker's people since the Wesleyans were already there. Jonker promised that he would not allow the Wesleyans to work among his people anymore, but rather would allow Kleinschmidt to come back.

Kleinschmidt came back and brought with him Hugo Hahn. They arrived in Windhoek (/Ai-//Gams) on December 9, 1842. They called the current Klein-Windhoek "Elberfeld" and Windhoek, "Barmen." The population of Windhoek was approximately 1,000 people.

In January 1843 the Herero chiefs Tjamuaha and Kahitjene made peace with Jonker Afrikaner ("The Peace of Windhoek"). This event provided a good opportunity for the missionaries. In February Hugo Hahn was able to visit the Ovaherero of Okahandja for the first time and was well received. Other chiefs to the south of Windhoek were willing to accept missionaries to work among their people.

Soon however the "Peace of Windhoek" was disturbed. The coming of the two Wesleyan missionaries, Haddy and Tindall, to Windhoek in 1844 was one of the factors. Chief Jonker Afrikaner, who had promised Kleinschmidt that he would not allow the Wesleyans to work among his people, was no longer prepared to keep that promise. He wanted, rather, to keep all four missionaries—the two from the RMS and the two Wesleyans. Jonker wanted to be at peace with his brothers in Warmbad and along the banks of the Orange River. They wanted union with him on the condition that he allow their missionaries (the Wesleyans of Warmbad) to work among his people. For Jonker to break his promise was both a diplomatic action and a political compromise for the sake of peace. Because of theological and methodological differences, however, the RMS refused to work with the Wesleyans. In October 1844 the RMS left Windhoek and established a mission station at Otjikango among the Herero.

To complicate matters, traders with goods and strong liquor also came to Windhoek. Chief Jonker bought many goods from them, including liquor, which he found himself unable to pay for. This led him to send out cattle-stealing expeditions to the Herero. The "Peace of Windhoek" was thus broken between the Herero and the Nama. Jonker was no longer controllable. He plundered the territory as far as Ovamboland in 1860. Before his death on October 18, 1861 at Okahandja, he made peace with Tjamuaha and warned his son Christian to live in peace with Maharero, Tjamuaha's son. In the meantime, the Wesleyans left Windhoek in 1846. It was not long until the Seven Years War (1863–70) between the Herero and Nama broke out. It also affected the mission work. It was ended with the "Peace of Okahandja" of September 23, 1870. After the war, mission work in Windhoek was resumed by Johann Georg Schroder in 1871.

The mission work and national peace were also affected by the German-Namibian wars of colonial resistance between 1891 and 1909. Because of the importation of European weapons, many people were maimed.

After the war many people flocked to the church for baptism. This was also true after the First World War. In 1923 the membership of the Windhoek congregation alone was 10,123, among them 1,200 Ovambo.[23]

After the RMS entered Namibia, it quickly monopolized the country. At the time the Wesleyan mission stations were given into the responsibility of the RMS; the Society already had a string of mission stations in Hereroland and Namaland. They were: Bethanie (1842), Windhoek (1842), Otjikango (1844), Rehoboth (1845), Otjimbingwe (1849), Okahandja (1850), Berseba (1850), Gobabis (1856), Gibeon (1863), Keetmanshoop (Swartmodder) (1866), and

Warmbad (1867). They later established Omaruru (1870), Okombahe (1871), Waterberg (1873), Rietfontein (1885), Gaub (1895),
Karibib (1902), Swakopmund (1905), Lüderitz (1905), Usakos
(1907), Tsumeb (1907), Grootfontein (1910). Otjizasu, Otjizeva, Ot-
jihaenena, Okazeva, Sesfontein, Kamanjab, Fransfontein, Outjo and
many others were also founded before or soon after 1910.

Although the number of mission stations may seem to suggest
that people accepted Christianity with open arms, this was not always the case. Very often, the RMS missionaries collaborated with
the colonial governments. Faith was sometimes imposed on the people through violence, though "Faith is an act of the will and is not a
forced act. Conscience may be appealed to, it must not be constrained by violence."[24]

The missionaries were in favor of and, indeed, demanded the
black reserves, so that much of the country became the property of
the colonists and settlers.

The ulterior motive of the Mission in pressing for the establishment of reserves
is self-interest. The Society is seeking to obtain permanent safeguards for its
missionary work as well as for the means invested in the economic development of the country.[25]

Again, by establishing mission colonies (sendingkolonies):

The missionaries disrupted the way of life of the people, who needed to be con-
stantly on the move in order to seek out the best pastures for their stock, by
inducing them to settle permanently around their stations. Their indoctrina-
tion of the people in European culture and religion [philosophy of religion] also
introduced a new dependence on imported goods and a foreign ideology.[26]

The work of the RMS was not confined solely to the southern and
central parts of Namibia. In 1891 the Rhenish missionaries began
mission work in Ovamboland among the Kwanyama people who
live astride the Angolan and Namibian frontiers. Among the first
missionaries to Ovamboland were Friedrich Meisenholl, August
Wulfhorst ("Ashipala"), Hermann Tönjes, Heinrich Welsch, Albert
Hochstrate, Schar, and Schulte. They established mission stations at
Ondjiva, Omupanda, Namakunde, and Omatemba on the site of today's Angola. For about thirty years they labored among these people. The first baptism took place in 1895. Thirteen people entered the
faith. By the time they left, about 1,400 people had been baptized.
The New Testament was translated into the Oshikwanyama language. During the First World War, in 1917, the Portuguese expelled
these missionaries. Church elders Simson Shituwa (later ordained by

the Finnish Missionary Society) and Wilhelm Kafita shared the care of those left behind at mission stations.[27] In 1920 the RMS field in Uukwanyama (Ovamboland) was formally transferred to the Finnish Missionary Society (FMS), when Engela was founded as a Finnish mission station in Uukwanyama. After his ordination in 1925, Simson Shituwa was given his own congregation, in Endola, to organize. This he did.

Two Lutheran Churches were born out of the work of the RMS in Namibia, one for blacks and another for whites only. Separate racial development had also worked within the church. It was something designed not only to divide blacks from the whites, but also blacks from other blacks.

The Evangelical Lutheran Church in South West Africa (ELCSWA)

Commencing with the beginning of the Rhenish Mission in Namibia in 1842, many parochial and catechetical schools were established. The first baptism among the Herero, which took place after fifteen years of missions, was that of Uerieta Kazahendike (ca. 1835–1935), who was baptized as Johanna Maria on July 25, 1858 at Otjimbingwe. She was a Herero-Nama by tribe and later was married to Samuel Gertse. In 1866 a training school was established at Otjimbingwe ("Augustineum") for the training of indigenous teachers which later included training for evangelists. This school was mostly for the children (sons) of chiefs. Among the teachers were Hahn, Büttner, and Brincker. Some of the first students were Wilhelm Maharero, Petrus Tjeetjo, Josaphat Riarua, and Manasse Zeraua. The school was later transferred to Okahandja in 1890 under Gottlieb Viehe. Gustav Kamatoto, Daiv Zeraua, Leopold Mbaurama, and Frans Gertse were some of the first nine students at Okahandja.

There was no training for indigenous pastors to take the role of leadership in the church. Leadership responsibility was only for the missionaries. The mission's progress was significant between the two World Wars. The first synod was called in 1938. In the same year a theological seminary for evangelists and future pastors was opened. By 1955 it was reported:

The leadership of the work still is in the hands of the mission. Earnest efforts however are being made to lay a foundation for the formation of a young church. A great effort is being put forth for the training of pastors and evangelists in Karibib.[28]

The first indigenous pastors of the Rhenish Mission were ordained in 1949. Eight years later, the church was able to be autonomous. On October 4, 1957 it was constituted as the "Evangelical Lutheran Church in South West Africa" (Rhenish Mission Church), although originally the union churches (one of the three member churches of EKD) in Germany were the mission's major sponsors.

The congregations of the Rhenish Mission in South West Africa were founded by missionaries sent out by a Mission Society combining the confessions of the Lutheran and the Reformed type. Although most of the missionaries sent out to South West Africa belonged to the Lutheran type, there has never been an outspoken Lutheran exclusiveness among them nor among the church-members. So long as the Mission Society had the responsibility for the spiritual guidance of all congregations, it seemed not so necessary to name the characteristic size of the whole work. What was definitely clear, was that all congregations without exception used the Small Catechism of Dr. Martin Luther. The constitution of the church has been based on this fact and after thorough investigation the pastors themselves decided that the name of the church must be "Evangelical Lutheran", based on the Small Catechism and the Augsburg Confession. . . . It was a surprise to the whole church that opposition arose toward the name.[29]

The opposition was raised by the Rehoboth Basters, who feared that the special rights given them by the government and the identity of the church would be lost by the move and name of the new church. Another issue was the right of property. The Rhenish Mission had a special relationship with the Basters and promised them the Mission property in the case that the Mission be relinquished. Again, according to the laws of the land, Basters, unlike other "non-whites," were entitled to own real estate. On the other hand, the Basters knew that the white Germans were not ready to join the new ELCSWA. If there was a German Church, why could there not be a Basters or Coloured Church? Nevertheless, the name was never changed and the Basters did not join. Some formed their own church, as we shall see below.

The Rev. H. K. Diehl was the first *Präses* (President) of the ELCSWA. He held this office for fifteen years (1957–72). The second *Präses* was Dr. J. L. de Vries (1973–78). Hendrik Frederik became the third *Präses* in 1979 and was the first to bear the title of "bishop" of that church on May 18, 1986. Today the membership of the Evangelical Lutheran Church in South West Africa is 193,000.

This church is a member of the Lutheran World Federation (LWF), the Federation of the Evangelical Lutheran Churches in Southern Africa (FELCSA), the United Evangelical Lutheran Churches in South West Africa (UELCSWA), and the Council of Churches in Namibia (CCN). It is in charge of Martin Luther High School and jointly sponsors the United Theological Seminary at Otjimbingwe with the black sister church, the Evangelical Lutheran Church in Namibia (ELCIN).

THE GERMAN EVANGELICAL LUTHERAN CHURCH (DELK)

The Lutheran Churches in Namibia exist on racial lines. Although the formation of the ELCSWA was based on a non-racial understanding, opposition to its formation came not only from the Rehobothers, but, even more strongly, from the white Germans who did not want to join together in one body with blacks. They, as "non-blacks," did not want to hold communion with the "non-whites." The Rhenish Mission missionaries worked also among the German-speaking Namibians. However, "they did not consider their work among the whites as missionary work in comparison to their work among the black people."[30]

The early missionaries were saddled almost overnight with the spiritual care of also the German garrison and colonists—white German soldiers, farmers and businessmen . . . as missionaries to the natives, on the other hand, and as spiritual shepherd or pastor to the growing white German community on the other. . . .[31]

The German community did not feel equal to the black community. Therefore, they preferred to stay as a white church, whatever name they were going to adopt in the future. In 1926 the German community established a synod and formally constituted themselves the "German Evangelical Lutheran Church in South West Africa" in 1960.

In 1960 the various congregations of the white German community joined forces and became an exclusively identifiable church, the German Evangelical Lutheran Church (DELK), whereas the non-white converts of the early missionaries and their descendants got their "own" church, the Evangelical Lutheran Church in South West Africa (Rhenish Mission Church: ELK), the latter becoming constitutionally independent in 1957. Thus, although along different paths, the South African Dutch Reformed Church and the South West African Lutheran Church seem to have attained the same end-result: a church clearly and cleanly divided along racialistic or skin-deep lines. . . .[32]

Three years later DELK received LWF membership status. By then its membership was reported to be 18,000, according to the application to the LWF. But the statistics of LWF of 1986 show the DELK membership as being 12,000. The number of members reported at the time of application may have been wrong or many Germans left Namibia in the meantime.

Although this church is in Namibia, it is hard to categorize it as a Namibian church. This is not only because of the name "German" connected to it, but also because its pastors and leaders are mostly not Namibians—they come from Germany. The church has a contractual relationship with the foreign office of the Evangelical Church in Germany (EKD), which is comprised of the Lutherans (VELKD), the Union, and the Reformed Churches. Only some member churches of the EKD are members of the LWF.

For many years this church (DELK) has preferred a *status quo* in the midst of Namibian political, economic and social issues. DELK has been hesitant or has even refused to participate in matters of concern with sister black Lutheran Churches in the country. This was evident at the time that the two black Lutheran Churches joined together in the federation known as the "United Evangelical Lutheran Churches in South West Africa" (UELCSWA) as a body hoping for future total union of all Lutheran churches in the country into one church across races. "Originally the German ELCSWA hesitated to join UELCSWA because of its socio-political witness in the Namibia crisis."[33] It seems the rule of the church and the understanding of the gospel in society has been and probably still is differently understood between black and white Lutherans in Namibia. It is not only a matter of socio-political witness and participation, but also the way theology is contextually interpreted. Lukas de Vries, one of the former leading black Namibian theologians, once said:

Western theology is unilaterally adjusted to the "spiritual freedom" and obedience, and has lost the biblical connotation of the "liberation from the circumstances of outward slavery". Western theology cannot liberate the blacks from slavery, inferiority complexes, distrust against oneself and the continuing dependence on others which lead to self-hate. . . . Political non-involvement and indifference in a society of oppression and brutality is as much a sin as murder, for this contributes to the growth of such unjust practices.[34]

The German ELCSWA applied for UELCSWA membership in 1975, but it was accepted only after some years when that church withdrew its objection to the declared aim of UELCSWA "to strive

. . . for full unity and merger of the Lutheran churches in Namibia." But the church's stand of political neutrality and of non-social involvement continues to prevail. As a result, in 1984 this church, together with a sister church in South Africa, was suspended from the LWF at Budapest, Hungary. The Seventh Assembly of the Lutheran World Federation adopted that it:

> . . . *Strongly and urgently appeals* to its white member churches in Southern Africa, namely the Evangelical Lutheran Church in Southern Africa (Cape Church) and the German Evangelical Lutheran Church in South West Africa (Namibia) to publicly and unequivocally reject the system of apartheid (separate development) and to end the division of the church on racial grounds. . . .
> The Assembly is constrained to SUSPEND THE MEMBERSHIP of the above churches, intending that such action serve as a help for those churches to come to clear witness against the policy of apartheid . . . and to move to visible unity of the Lutheran churches in Southern Africa . . . understands that suspension means that those churches are not entitled to send voting delegates to an LWF Assembly or official meeting, nor to have any of their members on a governing organ of the Federation.[35]

More than ever before, the German Church in Namibia has joined other Namibian Lutheran Churches in denouncing the policy of segregation. The three Lutheran Churches in Namibia have expressed a joint willingness to merge as one Lutheran Church by 1992. Today (since 1986), the President of the German Church in Namibia is also the President of UELCSWA. DELK is a member of UELCSWA, CCN, FELCSA, UELCSA and LWF.

Hugo Hahn and Johannes Rath were among the pioneering pillars in the establishment of the Rhenish Mission Society in Namibia. One hundred and forty-four years have passed since the advent of the Rhenish mission in Namibia in 1842. The church will not be independent until the whole nation is independent. Although these churches are no longer mission fields, they still need foreign support and assistance to make their years of independence a reality. This independence will be seen through their own self-support, self-government, self-propagation through theology and preaching which is contextual but also globally concerned at the same time.

THE FINNISH MISSIONARY SOCIETY (FMS)

Less is known of the early history of Finland than of any other European country. The pagan inhabitants were governed by their own kings until the middle of the 12th century, when their piracies provoked Sweden to undertake a crusade against them, at the same time introducing Christianity and planting some colonies among them, thus acquiring a hold on Finland which was retained for several centuries.[36]

As Christianity was introduced to Germany in the eighth century, Chrisitanity was accepted in Finland by the twelfth century.

Finland was the last of the northern nations to receive Christianity. This came about in 1157 through the Swedish King Erik, the Holy, and the Upsala Bishop Henrik. It was likewise the last of the northern nations to take up the heathen mission work.[37]

Finland underwent a general religious awakening between 1820 and 1830.[38] The establishment of the missionary society in Sweden in 1835 caused many Finns to think of unchristian peoples and they desired to organize a similar society. Chaplain Jonas Lagus of Yliewiska bought a home which he dedicated to be used as a mission school. In 1837 Jonas travelled to Stockholm to study the strategies of the Swedish Missionary Society. He then visited southern Finland to awaken interest in missions. Finnish pastors also collected missionary offerings and sent part of them to the Swedish Mission. Little circles of the Finn Mission Friends contributed sums of money to the Swedish Society.

On January 19, 1857 Finland celebrated the seven hundredth anniversary of its christianization. It was on this date and occasion that the Finnish Missionary Society was founded. Professor F. L. Schauman was its first director. This society contributed to the mission work of the Leipzig and Gossner Mission Societies in Hermannsburg and Berlin, respectively. From 1860, the Finns supported the German foreign mission work with both money and personnel. A Finn, Malmström, was ordained in 1866 and was sent to the Hermannsburg station, Matleb, South Africa. Malmström operated under the auspices of the Rhenish Mission; however, "The Finland Society was to support this station, and all the information was to be sent to Finland."[39] K. E. Jurvelin was also working under the Rhenish Mission. We shall meet these two men again later. This connection created a wish among some Finns to work in Africa.

Although the FMS was established as the missionary organ of the national church—the Evangelical Lutheran Church of Finland—it was, nevertheless, a free society.[40]

It was noted above that Carl Hugo Hahn[41] of the Rhenish Mission visited Ovamboland in 1857 and 1866. It was on his second visit (1866) to Ovamboland that King Shikongo shaKalulu of Ondonga and King Mweshipandeka shaShaningika of Uukwanyama asked

Hahn to send missionaries to them. Before his second visit to Ovamboland Hahn was in Europe (1859–63) to organize financial support for the mission. He travelled extensively in Germany, England and Russia. In 1862 Hahn lectured in Helsingfors, Finland, about his journey to Ovamboland and his work among the Herero. The lecture impressed the Finns and roused more interest in Africa. As a result of that lecture Finns sent the sum of 863 k. to Hahn's school in Namibia (Hereroland) in 1863 to educate the indigenous preachers.[42]

After his second visit to Ovamboland in 1866—where he visited Ondonga, Uukwanyama, Uukwaluudhi and Ongandjera—Hahn sent a letter, along with a diary of his journey, to the FMS, urging them to come in order to help him and his colleagues. He wrote:

This will tell you, the Finnish Mission Society, it is time you remember your promise to come over and help us. Trusting that this request will not be denied, I come to you in God's name, who wills that all shall be saved; and in our Lutheran Mission's name, that is so little known in this land; and in the poor heathen's name, to whom God has opened the door, and ordered me to speak. "Come over and help." I have, in God's name, dared to give three tribes the promise that before two years they shall have missionaries and Christian workers.[43]

In 1867 the FMS considered whether or not to accept the invitation to Ovamboland. On account of the letter, in an extra meeting the directors of the Society decided on September 18, 1867 to send missionaries to Ovamboland.

In 1867 the Finnish Mission Society had to decide if it will take the call to go to Ovamboland. There were many frightening things. . . . On September 18, 1867 at the extra meeting of the Society, it was decided upon to send its missionaries to the Ovambo people. The same year was also the final year of those who attended the first missionary school. These men eventually became an answer to the call of [King] Shikongo shaKalulu.[44]

On December 31, 1868[45] the first group of nine Finnish missionaries arrived in Cape Town. They included Erkki Juntunen and/or Juho Nissinen, Martti Rautanen (Nakambalekanene, meaning "Big Head-hat," "Old Hat-head" or "Uncle Nakambale"), Juho Heinone, Antti Piirainen, Karl L. Tolonen, Botolf B. Björklund, Karl A. Veikkolin, and Pietari Kurvinen. Not all of them were ordained pastors. It was said that "five students of their mission school and three colonists were commissioned for Ovambo."[46] This statement was made regarding their departure from Finland because they stopped in Germany, where they picked up the ninth man.[47]

At the Cape they were met by an old Rhenish missionary, P. D. Lückhoff. The same day, January 1, 1869, they went as far as Stellenbosch to meet with the Director of the Rhenish Society, C. H. Ritter.[48] On February 1, 1869 they returned to Cape Town and met with Bishop R. Grey of the Anglican Church. The group, joined by Malmström,[49] who was then working in South Africa, now numbered ten. It departed Cape Town by boat for Walvis Bay on February 4, 1869. Ten days later, the missionaries arrived in the Namibian port. It was at Walvis Bay that the missionary Carl Hugo Hahn met the group in early March. He eventually took them to his mission colony at Otjimbingwe, where they stayed for a year and a half to learn the Otjiherero, Dutch, and English languages. At times, in order to facilitate fluency in the lanuage those who were pastors were given the opportunity to preach to the Herero.

While at Otjimbingwe, the missionaries met the family of Heinrich Kleinschmidt. Two of them, Rautanen and Björklund, later married daughters of Kleinschmidt. Björklund married Katherina Albertina (Kitty), the oldest daughter, on March 5, 1874, and Rautanen married eighteen year old Anna Friederike (Frieda) on September 11, 1872.

FINNISH MISSION IN OVAMBOLAND

After their six ox wagons were fixed, the new missionaries were ready to take the journey to Ovamboland. The journey began on May 27, 1870. Tolonen remained behind for a while at Otjimbingwe. The trader Frederick Green was the leader of the missionary convoy to Ovamboland. On July 9, 1870 the first Finnish missionaries arrived at Omandongo near King Shikongo shaKalulu's palace of the Ondonga tribe (nation). They were well received by the king. It was here that the gospel was first preached. It then spread throughout the northern parts of Namibia. The 9th of July is observed by the Evangelical Lutheran Church in Namibia in commemoration of the missionaries' arrival.

The second group of missionaries from Finland arrived at Otjimbingwe in January 1871. This group included T. Reijonen, Gustav Mauritz Skoglund, and three girlfriends of the young missionaries. Reijonen and Skoglund were installed for mission work by Hugo Hahn of the Rhenish Mission at Otjimbingwe. Reijonen, Skoglund, Tolonen and the three women joined the rest of the first group in Ovamboland at that time.

Soon missionaries were to be found scattered all over Ovamboland, and many mission stations were established. From the beginning, Björklund served as their mission director, but eventually
Rautanen emerged as their "bishop."

Between 1870 and 1883 mission work was extended to
Uukwambi, Ongandjera and Uukwanyama. Mission stations established during this period were Omandongo (1870), Olukonda
(1871), Rehoboth (Okahao, 1871), Rikobo (mUukwambi, 1872),[50]
Oniipa (1873), Ondjumba (1873), Omulonga (1874). The indigenous residents were not always receptive, however, and by the end
of 1873 all missionaries were expelled from all other Ovambo tribal
lands except Ondongaland (among the Aadonga tribe). By 1880 the
missionaries Malmström, Jurvelin, Kurvinen and Tolonen had returned to Finland and never came back. Skoglund died in 1880. Piirainen went back to Hereroland at Omaruru, where he became a
trader. The death of Skoglund, who is buried at Omulonga in Ondonga, was a shock and a great loss to King Kambonde of Ondonga,
who said, "My heart and my head is full of tears; I cannot speak. He
was my true friend and helper, and I shall mourn him all my life."[51]
King Kambonde wanted his people to be taught new things.

For thirteen years the missionaries labored without any official
converts. The Ovambo, like all other Namibian indigenous people,
were skeptical, suspicious and antagonistic toward the missionaries'
real purpose and ultimate aim. They came to listen to the preaching,
but no one was publicly ready to commit himself or herself to baptism.

Through the patience and forbearance of these preachers of good
news, the first public baptism among the Ovambo took place on January 6, 1883 at Omulonga when six men—Moses Iimene, Elias
Nangolo, Abraham Shikongo, Jakob Angula, Tobias Negonya and
Johannes Nangombe—came forward for Holy Baptism. With them
was an infant, a child of Eva Maria, who was also baptized the same
day. In March of the same year three more people were baptized at
Omandongo.

It would be a mistake to consider this baptism the first among the
Ovambo people. It was at least the third or fourth. It was only the
first public one in Ovamboland. An Ovambo woman, Nanguroshi,
a servant to the missionary Kurvinen, accompanied him on his return to Finland in 1874. There in Helsinki, she was baptized on June
9, 1876.[52] Four years later she came back to Namibia, stayed in

Hereroland and later married one of the young Ovambo men who had been baptized by the Rhenish missionary G. Viehe on behalf of the Finnish missionaries at Omaruru in 1881. The four men were Gustav Iithoko, Wilhelm Amutenya, Martin Iipinage, and Gabriel Nangolo. It seems that besides the Africans' skepticism towards the missionaries, the Finnish missionaries were also careful not to rush to do a baptism until they were trusted by the people to do such a strange rite as that of pouring water on adults in public. Thirteen years without baptism should not be looked on from the point of view that the Africans were too "evil" and deep in their sin. It is natural for anyone to be skeptical of what others are saying, moreso if they are foreigners. It was recounted that:

At the end of the 1870s some of the Ovambo people had already requested for baptism. The missionaries, with full reasoins, were scared that [King] Kambonde might regard baptism as a punishable act. They sent the first four baptismal candidates who were all young men, to Omaruru where a German missionary, G. Viehe, baptised them on 6.3.1881 [March 6, 1881]. One of the four men came to see [King] Kambonde the following year. Although the man was unfriendly received, King Kambonde did not persecute him for him being baptised.

A significant advance was made in 1884 when four more people— Paulus (Omushimba), David (Niitembu), Elias (Ashikomba) and Elizabeth (Kaukaus)—were baptized at Olukonda.

During this period, Europeans were exporting large quantities of strong drink into Namibia, Ovamboland included. The Portuguese in Angola were trading slaves with the Ovambo kings and chiefs. Nevertheless, after 1883 the missionaries continued to evangelize, teach and translate the Scriptures and write small books in local languages for local usage. Unfortunately, the power struggle between the Ondonga kings—brothers Kambonde and Nehale Mpingana— started. They divided the Ondonga land. King Kambonde took the west and Nehale took the east. In about the 1890s King Nehale destroyed the Omulonga and Omandongo mission stations in the east of Ondonga (in his land). The missionaries left east Ondonga for a while and in 1890 established Ondangwa in west Ondonga to replace the two lost mission stations. At this time also, many missionaries had either died of malaria or gone back to South Africa or Finland. There was a time when only two missionaries were in the field. Nevertheless, King Kambonde kaMpingana, in west Ondonga, appealed to the FMS to send more missionaries.

Despite the missionaries' difficult lot, the few who had remained continued the work. In 1888 the first church building in the mission field was built at Olukonda. New missionaries August Pettinen and Albin Savola joined the staff. Progress was realized. In 1887, fifty-one people were baptized. The numbers of Christians were as follows:

Year	# of Christians	Year	# of Christians
1870	0	1930	23,126
1883	11	1940	35,732
1890	489	1950	63,451
1899	752	1960	118,316
1904	1,610	1970	194,884
1910	2,018	1980	300,000
1920	7,695	1986	350,266[54]
1926	19,309		

Some of the difficulties encountered and/or mistakes made in the mission field were in these matters: excessive usage of imported strong drink, the abolishment of initiation schools (*ohango*), the fear of twins, the cutting off of African decorated hairs (*oondjuhi*), and the abolishment of African clothing and musical instruments. Although people were forbidden to practice some of these things, they continued to practice in secret. Their customs rooted in the blood, they refused to accept what was imposed on them. The practices are still alive today. For example, the use of African drums was forbidden. Their usage has returned. It is expected that other native customs will also return in the future.

The six week visit of the Finnish Mission Society Director, Jooseppi Mustakallio, in 1900 was an important moment with regard to the mission field. It reestablished contact between the missionaries and their home country. Much support and help came from Finland because of this visit. New missionaries and professional teachers came to the field. Hilja Lindberg, for example, came to teach weaving. New stations were built: Ontananga (1900), Onayena (1902), Nakeke (1903), Ompupupu (1908), Rehoboth rebuilt (1908), Onashiku (1908), Elim (1908), Oshigambo (1908) and Tshandi (1909).

In 1912, on his deathbed, King Kambonde kaNgula (Eino Johannes) of Ondonga was the first Ovambo king to be baptized. On December 1 of the same year, his brother and successor, King Nambala (Martin Elifas) Kadhikwa (1894–1942), was also baptized, together with fifty-six other people, at Olukonda. The baptism of the king opened up another fruitful period for the missionaries. The first baptism in Uukwambi did not occur until 1912.

Abraham Iintamba, a local preacher from Ongandjera, was the first to take Christian preaching to Uukolonkadhi. From the beginning the RMS had made unsuccessful attempts to evangelize Uukwanyama. Nonetheless, it had been mainly a Rhenish mission field. The Finnish entered the area when the German missionaries were expelled from Uukwanyama by the Portuguese in 1917. However, it was not until 1921, through the work of Simson Shituwa and Wilhelm Kafita in conjunction with the English officials and the Finnish missionary Emil Liljeblad, that a Finnish station, Engela, in Uukwanyama was founded by August Hänninen from Oshigambo.

Unlike the Rhenish missionaries, the Finns opened up doors for African leadership early in their mission. They trained their local assistant teachers very early. For example, Gustav Iithoko (Shigwedha, ca. 1861–1916), who was from Oniihwa, Onayena and one of those baptized in 1881 at Omaruru, was made an elder at Omandongo in 1887. He was also a school teacher at Onamayi (not far from Onayena, 1893–97) and at Oyovu (not far from Oshigambo, 1898–1915). Because of famine, schools were closed and he left teaching to work in the south of Namibia, where he died in 1916.[55]

In 1913 the Teachers Training Seminary for men was opened at Oniipa with six students. All were from the Oniipa congregation. Liljeblad was its first headmaster. Johanna Kristof, the first Ovambo woman teacher, graduated in 1928. The same year girls' schools were also established at different places. The development of schools for girls was a slow process. Mrs. Anna Rautaheimo started educating fiancees of the boys in Teachers Training School at Onandjokwe in 1921. This school was later transferred to Oshigambo in 1924. The same year a similar school was established at Engela. Others followed at Tshandi, Elim, Oniimwandi, Okalongo, Ondobe, Omundaungilo, and also in Okavango. A boys' school ("Jongenskool") was founded at Engela by W. Kivinen in 1926. It was the responsibility of students to build their own classrooms since there were no funds available for school projects. In 1927 a technical school was opened at Ongwediva. It was not until 1947 that Teachers Training Seminary for women was begun at Okahao. To provide for adequate facilities and training and to cut short distances to schools for young people, it was necessary to establish boarding schools. Many of these kinds of schools were built. All, except one (the Oshigambo Secondary School, 1952), have today been taken over by the state.

Training for pastors and evangelists were begun in 1922 at Oniipa. Their first graduation was held in 1925. Seven became pastors while the remaining ten became evangelists. The first pastors were ordained on September 27, 1925. They were: Simson Shituwa, Juuso Ngaikukwete, Nabot Manasse, Obadja Iihuhwa, Sakeus Iihuhwa, Gideon Iitula and Paulus Hamutenya. After the graduation of the first local preachers, the number of Christians greatly increased—from 7,695 in 1920 to 19,309 in 1926. "It was [also] noticeable that more converts were made in times of famine or sickness. . . ."[56] In 1947 the theological seminary was moved to Elim, where it remained until 1962. The following year it was merged with the ELCSWA theological seminary at Otjimbingwe.

In 1952 the Engela Church Institute was established to train evangelists, catechetics, choir directors, Bible study group leaders, Sunday School teachers, and other necessary church workers. Meanwhile, the Finnish mission was concerned about the educational regulations enacted by the government in 1935.

These prescribe that no school may be within five miles of another school, that school buildings must be of brick, that every teacher must have a teacher's diploma, and that Afrikaans must be taught in every school. About three thousand children are affected, being in schools which do not conform to one or another of the regulations. Since schools do not draw any government grant, the Finnish mission resents the application of the government.[57]

These regulations were an attempt to impair and prevent the Finnish missionaries from improving black education and to impose the language of Afrikaans upon the children. The missionaries' intentions were based on equal education for all in any way possible. There was, on the other hand, neither money, transportation, nor schools to qualify accredited teachers or to meet the other demands of the government. This was also well known by the state.

At about the same time the government advised the Finnish mission not to use local preachers who did not have teacher's training or formal preaching education. This regulation had the same effect on the mission of the church as it had on education. Preaching was more open to all believers before the regulation, and growth of church membership was realized through such "uneducated" preachers.

A major stumbling block appeared en route of the spreading of the Gospel. The government prohibited the Mission to stop using people who never had a formal education as teachers or as preachers. This prohibition led to the closure of many schools because there were no people with formal education in teaching or preaching. Pastors were the only ones allowed to preach the Gospel in the villages.

The first doctor in Ovamboland was Dr. Selma Rainio, who arrived in 1908. Three years later Onandjokwe Hospital was established. The first printing press was founded at Oniipa in 1901 and published the church newspaper *Osondaha* the same year. This was the same church press which was bombed by "unknowns" in 1973 and 1980, another attempt having been made in 1982. *Omukwetu,* the church newspaper which replaced *Osondaha,* is published at Oniipa.

The Finnish Mission in Ovamboland assumed the name "The Order of the Evangelical Lutheran Church in Ovamboland" in 1924. Its first synod was called in 1925. The same year M. Rautanen was granted a D. Th. *honoris causa* degree by the University of Helsinki for his work in Ovamboland since 1870. The mission of the Finns was also extended to other regions.

FINNISH MISSION IN OKAVANGOLAND

Okavango is about 180 kilometers east of Ovamboland. The first Christians in Kavango (Okavango) are indebted to the Rhenish Mission, especially through the contract laborers in the south (Usimba).[59] The Roman Catholic Church worked in the region beginning in 1902, but more actively after 1914. Some people were Christians before the Finns entered the region. It was these few Christians who later invited the Finnish missionaries to start mission work in Kavango. In 1926 a Finn, Emil Närhi, visited Okavango with some Ovambo Christians. On April 30 of the same year Närhi baptized twenty-one people at Nkurenkuru,[60] though the mission station at Nkurenkuru was not established until 1929, by Aatu and Eetu Järvinen. Together with the Järvinens were three Ovambo teachers: Mateus Shininge, Elia Shanyengange,..and Samuel Shaanika. The following year Rupara and Mupini were established. Mpungu was established in 1963, Rundu in 1972, and the new congregation at Nepara after 1977.

Matias Shikondomboro was the first Okavango teacher. Later, in 1942, he was ordained a pastor. He received his education in Ovamboland and was sent to serve Rupara congregation. To make communication easier between Ovambo congregations and Okavango, the Okavango Circuit was formed in 1950. In 1938 the first girls' school ("Okagumbo") was founded at Nkurenkuru by Anna Rautaheimo. It was continued by Ms. Markkanen in 1940. Many Okavango students studied in Ovamboland.

FINNISH MISSION IN KAOKOVELD

It was natural for the people of Kaokoveld to visit their relatives in the central parts of Namibia and southern Angola. Therefore, they came into contact with German missionaries and some were baptized. However, in the Kaokoveld there was no one to serve these few Christians. They asked the Finnish missionaries in Ovamboland to come and preach to them and teach their children.

Sulo Aarni,[61] who worked at Tshandi for many years (1909–46), visited Kaokoveld time and again and offered services to the Christians in Kaoko. Obadja Iihuhwa, one of the first ordained local pastors, was sent to serve in Uukolonkadhi. He was also given a duty to minister to the Kaokolanders, when he could. In 1930 an Ovambo teacher was sent there, but he did not stay long.[62] By 1934 the Finns ended their attempts to establish a mission station in Kaokoveld. The reason for this abandonment, it seems, was lack of interest in the church by the Kaoko people. However, today the ELCIN inner mission is trying to revive the Kaoko mission and hopes to establish a congregation there in the near future.

FINNISH MISSION IN ANGOLA

The Angolan and Namibian frontier, occupied by the Ovambo, belonged to the Kwanyama tribe. It was among these Ovambo people of southern Angola and north of the Namibian border that the Rhenish Mission had been doing mission work since 1891. In 1920, after the expulsion of the Germans from Angola by the Portuguese, the field was transferred to the Finnish mission. Engela, within the border of Namibia, was established to replace the old Rhenish stations within Angola. It was established in 1921 to serve these former German converts.

In 1924 Nestor Wäänänen and some Ovambo Christians attempted unsuccessfully to get permission to work in Angola. It was reported that "Finnish missionaries, pioneering among the Ovambo in Angola, were eventually taken into the service of the [interdenominational] Swiss Philafrican Mission," which had entered Angola, its only field, in 1897.[63]

Again in 1932 a group of Ovambo teachers, including Martin Ndjembela (Hepeni), Filippus Kamati, Paulus Hamutenya, Vilho Kaulinge, Vilho Ueyulu, and H. Sheetekela, decided to evangelize the heathen both in Angola and in Namibia. The group, which went to Angola, included the following men: Filippus Shikwendule Kamati, Aaron Nghiishililwa, Andreas Nghiwete, Josef Mbinga, Wilhelm Londeinge, Lukas Namalemo, Abisalom Nangonya, Andreas Shafombabi, Tobias Haihonya and Josef Puleni. Among others, Kamati and Ndjembela suffered greatly. In 1933 Kamati was detained in Angola and died in a Portuguese cell. Before his death Kamati wrote a letter to the Christians at Engela congregation.

Ondjiva
30 June, 1933

To the beloved in Jesus Christ who live in the Evangelical Church of Jesus Christ at Engela, I greet you in the Lord.

Rejoice for my imprisonment in Jesus as I myself do rejoice for it. I have discussed with the official at Ondjiva, but I could not convince him. I was, therefore, detained because a Catholic wrote four letters to the same official.

[Filippus Kamati][64]

Ndjembela was also detained and expelled twice from Angola. Rev. Paulus Hamutenya worked for a short time among the Ovakwanyama and San of east Uukwanyama before he died in 1932. However, Simson Ndatipo, one of Ndjembela's students in Angola, was baptized and later became an ELCIN pastor. Two Finns, Tuure Vapaavouri and Matti Peltola, also worked in Angola between 1939 and 1946.[65]

Ndatipo had worked in Angola for many years and was later joined by a second pastor, Noa Ndeutapo, in 1963. The following year evangelists Toivo Moonde, Wilhelm Haikali and Petrus Haunini were sent to join the Angola staff. Later Erkki and Kaija Halme, Anni Väisälä, Ritva Marttala, Samuel Shininge, Immanuel Kamho, Titus Namunyekwa and Ruben Mwombelo increased the number of the missionaries. Noa Ndeutapo is today functioning as the Dean of the Circuit of southern Angola as it is under the care of the ELCIN.

THE EVANGELICAL LUTHERAN CHURCH IN NAMIBIA (ELCIN-ELOC)

The Evangelical Lutheran Ovambo-Kavango Church (ELOC) was constituted in 1954. It was recognized by the state in 1957. On June 20, 1963 the first indigenous pastor, Dr. Leonard Nangolo

Auala, born in 1908, became the first bishop of the ELOC (1963–78). He was followed in leadership by Dr. Kleopas Dumeni (1979-).

This church had its own theological seminary to train pastors and evangelists, first at Oniipa (1922–46), then at Elim (1947–62). In 1963 this seminary and that of the Evangelical Lutheran Church in South West Africa/Namibia (ELCSWA) were united and became known as the United Lutheran Theological Seminary in Namibia (Paulinum) at Otjimbingwe. Its inauguration took place on June 16, 1963. The ELOC also had a preparatory course for pastors at Oshigambo (1953–59). That course was intended to bring the students to the level of standard eight qualification; this standard was not begun at Oshigambo until 1960.

Due to the hope of a future merger with other Lutheran Churches in the country and to create a sense of nationhood, it was considered necessary to change the name, which was intended to cover the areas of Ovambo and Okavango and to get away from a tribally oriented name. The name "Evangelical Lutheran Church in Namibia" (ELCIN) was, therefore, adopted at the Synod of 1984 to replace the old name, "Evangelical Lutheran Ovambo-Kavango Church" (ELOC). As a result, there are two Lutheran Churches in Namibia with the same name, i.e., the Evangelical Lutheran Church in South West Africa (ELCSWA-Rhenish Mission)[66] and the Evangelical Lutheran Church in Namibia (ELCIN-ELOC, Finnish Mission). The membership of ELCSWA in 1986 was 193,000 and that of ELCIN was 350,266.

THE ROMAN CATHOLIC CHURCH

Many Catholic religious orders and missionary societies worked in Africa. They included the White Fathers, Holy Ghost Fathers, Franciscans, Dominicans, and Trinitarians. The orders which worked in Namibia were the Oblates of Mary Immaculate (OMI), who came from Hunfeld in Germany, assisted by the Holy Cross Sisters and Benedictine Sisters, the Holy Ghost Fathers and the Oblates of St. Francis de Sales (Salestians—OSFS).

The Benedictine Order was founded by St. Benedict of Nursia in 529. Its rule was "practical and provided for manuel labor by the monks as well as study and contemplation."[67] That of the Oblates of St. Francis de Sales was founded at Troyes, France in 1872. In 1882 the Oblates of St. Francis de Sales came to Africa and assumed charge of the mission stations in Namaland south of the Orange River. The

Oblates of the Immaculate Virgin Mary was founded in France on December 17, 1893 with this motto: "*Evangelizare pauperibus misit me.*" The Holy Ghost Fathers were founded in 1703 by Claude Francois Poullart des Places to train students for pastoral work in Paris. In 1848 they were united and became known as "The Congregation of the Holy Ghost" (CSSp). The Jesuits organized the congregation for the Propaganda of the Faith in Rome in 1622. In 1865 the Propaganda was requested to assign the CSSp to Angola. This led to eventual attempts by the Jesuits to found mission stations in Namibia.

It should be noted that in dealing with the Roman Catholic Church, racial lines are less emphasized. They are emphasized much more among the Protestant Churches. Du Plessis put it this way:

> . . . It is exceptionally difficult to differentiate between work among Europeans and missions to natives. No separate statistics are provided. Mission work, in the sense in which the term is used by Protestant Churches and Societies, is unknown in the Roman Church.[68]

Of course, such a distinction can be seen in situations and contexts where one race is most represented. However, some feel that the Roman Church has played a neutral role and has not clearly expressed its true position with regard to racial lines.[69]

The Prefecture of Cimbebasia

The story of the beginning of the Roman Catholic Church in Namibia is complicated due to the lack of well organized material at our disposal. Sustained Catholic influence was not felt in Namibia until the end of the nineteenth century despite the fact that the Portuguese had reached the Namibian coast as early as 1484.

There was a time when three European governments— Portuguese, British, and German—claimed parts of Namibia at the same time in conjunction with their missionaries. The Catholic Bishop Grimley secretly suggested to Napoleon III that he make a claim on the territory.[70] To show one of its results, Brown writes:

> . . . It was often difficult for missionaries to be sure what authorities they would have to negotiate with even though a formal agreement had been published in Europe before they set out. The whole of Damaraland . . . was believed to be a British Protectorate in 1879, but when a mission of the Holy Ghost Fathers reached Ovamboland two years later, they found that the Portuguese claim had been conceded.[71]

By the 1880s both Portugal and Britain recognized the country as a German Reich colony. It is worth noting that prior to 1820 the Roman Catholic Church was not permitted to do mission work in South Africa.[72] The first South African Vicariate of Cape Town was founded in 1837.[73] It was from this vicariate that the first attempts were made through Bishop Grimley to establish a Catholic mission in Namibia. According to Brown, the project was introduced to Bishop Grimley in this manner:

An Irish, Henry Edward Barry, wrote to Bishop Grimley in 1864 a lengthy account of the Damaras, *Namas, Twanas* and Matabeles, and urged the opportunity for missionary work among them. Since these peoples dwelt north of the Orange River, and so beyond the bounds of his vicariate, the bishop forwarded the information to Cardinal Barnabo, Prefect of Propaganda, who wrote to the Congregation of the Holy Ghost in terms which gave them the impression that the whole vast territory was to be added to their vicariate of the Two Guineas.[74] This impression was probably confirmed when Bishop Grimley at the Vatican Council approached their superior with the suggestion that the Holy Ghost Fathers should take over the northern part of his vicariate, including, if they so wished, Little Namaqualand.[75]

In fact, the Catholic mission in Little Namaland south of the Orange River was not well established until 1882. Little was done in the north beyond the river, although the Protestants had been working there since 1805. Father Charles Duparquet of the Congregation of the Holy Ghost in Angola[76] was sent on a tour of investigation in 1878 by his Superior-General.[77] He was to approach the people between the Orange and Kunene Rivers and discuss with them the possibilities of founding a mission station. He went first to Cape Town, where he again took a boat to Walvis Bay. He established a mission station in 1879 at Omaruru. When the Prefecture of Cimbebasia for the Congregation of the Holy Ghost was established by Cardinal Barnabo in 1879, Duparquet became the Vice-Prefect. The Prefecture Apostolic of Cimbebasia included Cassinga, then Caconda, Bihe, Massaca, and north and central Namibia and reached almost as far as the basin of the Upper Zambezi.[78] Father Duparquet, as its Vice-Prefect, installed Father Hogan and Brother Onophrios at Omaruru to work in the Walvis Bay area.[79] Part of Father Duparquet's responsibility was to travel throughout Damaraland and Ovamboland and get acquainted with the territory.

The Catholic mission, like all others, was aimed at the conversion of the Africans. In their propagation of the gospel the Catholics encountered many difficulties during those early days, including government prohibitions against working on the existing Protestant mission fields.[80] In addition to these internal difficulties, the French

Revolution (1787–99) also affected the missionary work of the Catholic Church "which had been directed and recruited, in the eighteenth century, from France and Portugal."[81] The Protestant missionary societies in the country, especially the Rhenish and the Finnish after they won some friendly relationship with the Africans, tried to instigate and persuade the kings and chiefs to exclude Catholics or even to expel them. The Catholic expulsion from Omaruru was related to these actions. Similar cases occurred both in Hereroland and Ovamboland.

When the Herero drove the Holy Ghost Fathers from Omaruru, two of them with some of their converts fled to the north of the Prefecture inside Angola. But there Father Delpuech and Brother Lucius were killed by the Ovambo in 1885. This led the Portuguese government in Angola to send its garrison to the northern banks of the Kunene River, while the Germans in Namibia commanded theirs to keep position. The Congregation of the Holy Ghost abandoned the Prefecture of Cimbebasia in 1888.[82] The southern part of Namibia was handed over to the Oblates of St. Francis de Sales, while the Oblates of Mary Immaculate were entrusted with the northern portion. The result of this division was the two Catholic vicariates—the Vicariate of Windhoek, which stretches from just south of Windhoek to the northern border, and the Vicariate of Keetmanshoop, which covers the rest of the country in the south.

THE VICARIATE OF KEETMANSHOOP

Although material on this topic is not available, the following can be said. When the Prefecture of Cimbebasia was abandoned, Bishop Simon of the Diocese of the Cape was ready to take over the area as it was entrusted to his Oblates of St. Francis de Sales, which had been working among the Nama south of the Orange River since 1882. The bishop travelled to Namibia to discuss the matter with the local chiefs and German officials, but he was refused permission to start a Catholic mission there. The blank refusal was based on the ground that it would divide the people. The Oblates were French and from English territory, whereas the Namibians were under German "protection" and also under the authority of Protestant missions. To permit the Catholics to start a mission would be against the treaty of the Namibians and Germans.[83]

From about 1888, Father Simon attempted unsuccessfully to establish a mission in Namibia every two years or so. Finally, he was given the right to buy a farm called Hierachabis in Namaland which was reorganized as a mission field. To make the Catholic mission a little easier, Bishop Simon thought it would be better if German Catholics were entrusted with the mission since the German government was in charge of the territory. Bishop Simon, therefore, urged Rome to form a separate prefecture of the area to be entrusted to the care of the Oblates of St. Francis de Sales of the German province. This proposal was accepted. On July 7, 1909, four years after the imperial orders granted freedom of founding missions to all churches, the Prefecture of Great Namaland was erected under the Salesians from the so-called "Austrian province." It became a vicariate in 1930. In 1949 this vicariate was elevated to a Vicariate of Keetmanshoop with its own bishop. An American, Edward J. Schlotterback, was a bishop of this vicariate. By 1975 it had sixteen congregations with a membership of 20,400 people.

THE VICARIATE OF WINDHOEK

When the Holy Ghost Fathers requested relief from the Prefecture of Cimbebasia, the area from Windhoek to the north, including southern Angola, was entrusted to the Oblates of Mary Immaculate, "who were in the process of forming a German province" in 1892.[84] However, the Oblates did not begin their work until 1896. Father A. Schoch, Prefect Apostolic of the Transvaal, managed to get a mission site from German officials. The same year two priests and a lay brother were sent to this mission field. In 1921 it was simply known as Cimbebasia Prefecture. Five years later it became the Vicariate of Windhoek.[85]

Although these missionaries were Germans, difficulties were not eliminated. At this time the country was under the monopoly of the Rhenish and Finnish Protestant missions. As a general rule, since the time of earlier Catholic missionaries in the country, the arrangement between those missions and the government was that no Catholics should be allowed to cross the boundaries of the already established mission fields. To maintain this arrangement, the Catholic Oblates were only permitted to minister to German Catholic settlers at Windhoek in 1896. Two years later another mission or Catholic parish was founded at Swakopmund. In 1902 the Aminius mission station was founded where some four hundred to five hundred Tswana people had just settled. It is not clear whether or not the Catholics were directly doing mission work to the Tswana people at the time of the establishment of Aminius.

The Catholics experienced the difficulty of a shortage of priests in the Oblate German province. Funds for these missions were also lacking.

After the German-Herero war, the restrictions on Catholics were removed to a certain degree. The Catholic mission could now explore new possibilities. The work was then extended, still under some conditions, to the Basters and Tswanas. A few more priests joined the mission staff in the meantime, including five trained nurses of the German Franciscan nuns who came in 1904. The nurses worked first in the military hospital during the war and later joined a newly opened mission hospital at Windhoek.[86] Finally the restrictions on Catholics were removed entirely.

It should be mentioned, however, that despite the restrictions on the Catholic missions, their movements and explorations for possible future points of contact of establishing mission stations were not completely limited. They learned to familiarize themselves with the areas in the north, as we shall soon see.

THE APOSTOLIC VICARIAT WINDHOEK, ROMAN CATHOLIC MISSION OVAMBOLAND

Three unsuccessful attempts were made to establish a mission in Ovamboland in the late 1800s.[87] In 1896 Father Schoch—together with the hunter Erikson—travelled from Grootfontein to Ongandjera, where he was well received by King Shaanika. The following year Father Hermann also visited Ongandjera.

In the early 1900s other unsuccessful attempts were made to Okavango. In 1903 Fathers Riegner, Filliung, and Hermandung reached Okavango, but they were not received by the king. One of them died of disease on the way. Four years later two priests, Krist and Lauer, and three indigenous people set out from Windhoek to Okavango, making Grootfontein their base. Although they tried twice, they did not reach their destination.[88] However, the fourth visit to Okavango, in 1909, was a success and King Libebe received them. Unfortunately, because of disease, several lives were lost in this venture. Father Gotthard and five other priests reached Okavango in 1910 and founded Nyangana in May 1911. Andara was founded in 1913, Tondoro in 1926, Bunya in 1928 and Sambiu in 1930. Many bush schools were erected. Teachers were sent to Windhoek for training. The mission was extended even to East Caprivi, where parishes, schools and a hospital were established.

It should be mentioned in regard to the extension of mission to Ovamboland that in 1900 two priests went to Otavi and then to Ovamboland. Because of restrictions, they could not do much. The Catholic Church newspaper *Omukuni* reported it this way:

In 1902 Evangelical Christians commenced their mission work in Ongandjera, but we [the Catholics] were prohibited by the government to go there. From there the German laws never allowed the Catholics to go to Ovamboland. We, therefore, went to Okavango where five major mission centers were established.

At the same time many Ovambo contract laborers were baptized in the south, especially in the Tsumeb copper mine. These men had difficulties with church affiliation in Ovamboland since they were baptized by the Catholics and there was not a Catholic Church in that part of the country. In 1923 Bishop Josef Gotthard, accompanied by Father Schulte (Komakende) of Tsumeb, visited the baptized Catholics in Ovamboland. They went as far as Mupa in southern Angola, which was part of their designated area. African chiefs in Angola gave them a site to establish a mission, but the Windhoek government did not allow them to work across the border and denied them permission to go there.

In 1924 the Union Mandatory decided that Ovamboland should be divided into three zones for missionary purposes. It was to be divided among the Finnish Missionary Society, the Anglican Mission and the Catholics. While the Finns concentrated more in Ondonga, the Damara Mission (Anglican) was given permission to work among the Ovakwanyama of Uukwanyama. The Catholic Mission had to choose among Uukwambi, Ongandjera, Ombalantu, Uukwaluudhi, Uukolonkadhi and Eunda. They chose Uukwambi and Ongandjera.

In 1924 Fathers Otto Fuhrmann and Schulte (Komakende) went to Uukwambi and founded a mission at Otshikuku on August 15. At Otshikuku they found a number of Catholic Christians, including Saba Katambo and Tshikarepo, who had been baptized at Tsumeb years before. As a result it took them only fourteen months before the first six people were baptized in Ovamboland.

King Iipumbu promised to assist the missionaries in any way he could. He also gave his two sons, Nuuyoma and Thikameni, to live with them at the mission station. Father Herman Bucking joined the new mission staff in October.

Although the Catholic Mission chose Ongandjera also, they did not go there. They went to Ombalantu instead, where Chief Kalipi kaSekusindi gave them Anamulenge. It appears that King Shaanika shaNashilongo of Ongandjera was no longer prepared to receive missionaries besides the Finnish Lutherans.[90] The suspicion was the traditional resentment of the Protestants.

In Ovamboland attempts were nevertheless made to visit southern Angola and meet other missionaries at Humbe. These Fathers also tried to follow up with the Catholics who were baptized at Tsumeb throughout the region as far as Namakunde inside Angola. Ten months later, hardworking Otto Fuhrmann (1895–1925) died of excessive work. Four Fathers—Antonius Wisskirchen, Johannes Helfrich, Kalush Kress (+1961) and B. Laub—joined the only remaining personnel, Herman Bucking, in 1927. The same year Wisskirchen founded Anamulenge, and Helfrich established Okatana in 1932. Four sisters also joined the Ovamboland mission staff in 1927. They were: Sr. Herluka (Niita), Sr. Emiliana, Sr. Germana, and St. Reginalda. They were the first missionary sisters in the area. Ovambo Catholic teachers, like those from Okavango, were also trained in Windhoek.

In 1927 the Roman Catholic school was established at Oniimwandi with Primus Eeru, the son of headman Eeru of Otshikuku, as its first teacher. A congregation was later founded at the same place. Another school was erected at Otshikutshatshipya the same year, with Albinus Atshipara as its first teacher. Faustinus Ambidhi taught school at Onampira beginning in 1930. Six years later a parish was also established at Onampira. Catholic schools and parishes were established in Uukwanatshikare (1929), Okando (1932), Ohetayi, Okambembe, and Iikokora. Wherever a school was erected, a congregation followed soon thereafter.

Sisterhood for the indigenous girls, "The Congregation of Native Sisters of St. Benedict under the Patronage of the Everblessed and Immaculate Virgin Mary," was established at Otshikuku in 1934. Otshikuku, Anamulenge (Ombalanbu), and Okatana had become the three major Roman Catholic stations in Ovamboland by 1945.

The Roman Catholic mission development throughout the country was so rapid that schools, clinics, hospitals and mission stations were established at many places in a very short time. These were all useful instruments in the extension of the church, but in the future these institutions were to create some problems. There were too many of them, with few facilities and not enough workers to run them.

Church leadership, as was always the case with Namibian missions, had been in the hands of the missionaries for a long time. It was not until 1942 that the first native, Gerard Molelekwa, was ordained. The second was Edward Kangootui, ordained in 1946, while Romanus Kampungo from Okavango became the third priest in 1951. The vicariate has an indigenous bishop, Bonifatius Haushiku, who was consecrated on January 27, 1979. This vicariate has been a full member of the Council of Churches in Namibia since 1982.

In 1975 the Catholic newspaper *Omukuni* recorded the statistics of the Catholics' two vicariates' membership as follows:

The Vicariate of Windhoek		The Vicariate of Keetmanshoop	
Andara	4,396	Aranos	1,059
Nyangana	5,711	Aroab	1,113
Rundu	2,274	Bathanien	485
Sambiu	6,814	Gabis	249
Bunya	8,758	Gibeon	2,086
Tondoro	6,104	Heirachabis	939
Okatana	13,787	Karasburg	2,200
Otshikuku	16,137	Keetmanshoop	3,747
Ombalantu	9,800	Lüderitz	1,522
Tsumeb	900	Mariental	708
Grootfontein	1,931	Oranjemund	1,291
Otavi	172	Rehoboth	2,510
St. Michael	533	Stampriet	431
Outjo	1,029	Tses	630
Otjiwarongo	3,174	Warmbad	707
Khorixas	1,451	Witkrans	723
Omaruru	1,349		
Waldfrieden	476	TOTAL	20,400
Karibib	202		
Goas	408		
Usakos	726		
Swakopmund	1,004		
Walvis Bay	2,400		
Okahandja	615		
Dobra	653		
Windhoek	7,848		
Witvlei	120		
Gobabis	4,220		
Gunichas	804		
Epukiro	2,060		
Aminius	2,310		
TOTAL	108,166		

108,166 + 20,400 = 128,566 = TOTAL Membership of 1974

By the early 1980s the combined work of the vicariates was described as 49 stations with 65 priests, 15 deacons, 29 brothers and more than 200 full- and part-time catechists. Teaching sisters numbered 277 and there were 21 brothers. In the schools, hospitals and clinics there were 541 teachers, five doctors and 584 nurses and helpers. It had 50 communities of nuns (convents) and chaplains to serve prisons and hospitals. There was also one Catholic priest, Gerhard Heimerikx (Kaishara, OMI), serving the exiled Namibians in African countries.

The church ran several institutions: (1) a press at Dobra, publisher of church literature and papers in several languages, including *Omukuni* newspaper; (2) fourteen kindergartens, 35 primary schools, 15 secondary schools, four advanced schools and a pastoral center; (3) forty-six primary and secondary school hostels; (4) thirteen hospitals and five clinics; and (5) an agricultural project in Okavango.

The Namibian Roman Catholic Church is a member of the Conference of Roman Catholic Bishops for Southern Africa, organized in 1952.

THE ANGLICAN CHURCH

After the annexation of Walvis Bay by Britain in 1878, priests of the Church of England from the Diocese of Cape Town visited the port from time to time to offer spiritual care to the Englishmen who were there.

But the desire of the Church of England to begin mission work in Namibia can be traced back to 1860 and Archbishop Gray of Cape Town. Gray wanted to work among the Ovambo.[91] Laurmaa reported the bishop to have said these words in 1878: "First of all we ought to go to those who are near us at the Kei river and to those who live in the northern and eastern regions; especially, we ought to go to the Owambo nations in the west."[92]

In 1883 it was decided to send C. F. Tobias to that mission, but the establishment of German protectorate over the territory in 1884 did not allow such a possibility.

In 1903 Bishop Alan G. S. Gibson of Cape Town was given permission by Governor Leutwein to visit Ovamboland.[93] In his story "Between Cape Town and Luanda" Gibson describes how he and his companions were well received by the Finnish missionary Pettinen and his family at Ondangwa. In their talks the Finns were eager to propose to the Church of England that it begin mission work among the Ovambo because the Finns had a shortage of both workers and finances. Once again, due to political suspicion and misgivings, the German government would not allow such a venture by the Anglicans. There was also a shortage of money for the Anglicans to start a mission at once.

As a consequence the Church of England had decided to serve only the English-speaking community. Unfortunately, except in Walvis Bay, there were no English-speaking persons anywhere in the country. In 1911 the Rev. F. M. C. Boehm, of German origin, visited the country for the purpose of establishing an Anglican mission, but he did not stay long.

The Anglican presence in Namibia was significantly established only after the collapse of German rule in Namibia in 1914–15. The establishment of the mandate that more English-speaking people come to Namibia, especially soldiers, government workers, and railway officials made it necessary to send English priests to minister to these people as chaplains. Archdeacon N. W. Fogarty was transferred to Windhoek from South Africa as a military chaplain. Confirmations had been conducted by Cape Town bishops during the early years of the Anglican Church in Namibia. In 1924 the army chaplain, Fogarty, became the first Anglican bishop of the newly established Diocese of Damaraland (Namibia). Anglican parishes in Windhoek—St. George's Cathedral and St. Barnabas—were built soon after. Others were erected at Keetmanshoop, Lüderitz, Usakos, Omaruru, Rehoboth, Swakopmund, Mariental, Aus, Gibeon, Karasburg, Ariamsvlei, Bethanie and Walvis Bay. St. George's Cathedral has been the seat of the Anglican bishops ever since.

THE OVAMBOLAND MISSION OF THE PROVINCE OF SOUTH AFRICA

Reference has been made to the fact that Archbishop Gray of "The Church of the Province of South Africa" or "Church of the Anglican Communion in South Africa" in Cape Town had a strong desire to begin a mission among the Ovambo people of Namibia. In 1923 negotiations were underway between Bishop Fogarty and Bishop Sidwell to send missionaries to Oukwanyama, in Ovamboland.

Meanwhile, in 1924, the Union Mandatory decided to divide Ovamboland into three zones—among the Finnish Missionary Society, Anglican Mission, and Catholic Mission. In June of the same year the Rev. G. W. R. Robias of Roodebloem, Cape Town, was sent to Oukwanyama as a missionary of the "The Ovamboland Mission of the Province of South Africa." The following year Tobias established St. Mary's Mission at Odibo, near state buildings and not far from the residence of one of the Oukwanyama chiefs. A hospital at St. Mary's, several bush schools (*eefikola domomikunda*), and preaching were the three elements in their missionary service. Mission stations were erected in various places, such as Onamunhama, Onamutayi and Oshandi. However, St. Mary's at Odibo and Holy Cross Mission at Oshandi, about twenty kilometers east of Odibo, were the major stations to which various outstations were attached.

The Anglican missionaries were educated to be both priests and teachers. Among those who should be mentioned are C. H. Bridges, W. E. Cawthorne, J. W. Adams, G. W. Dymond and Mr. Mac-Donald. Nevertheless, communication between the missionaries and indigenous people was not easy, simply because many English missionaries did not take pains to learn Oshikwanyama or other languages. It was necessary, therefore, to educate Africans for the purpose of serving as teachers and preachers. Despite the language factor, the mission flourished. One of the reasons was the work previously done in the region by other missionary societies. There were already many Ovakwanyama people who knew how to read and write, even if they were not Christians. Since the missionaries did not know Oshikwanyama, only a few books were produced and those were largely the work of the Ovakwanyama themselves.[94] The work was later extended outside of Oukwanyama.

The Anglican and Roman Catholic Missions were given only conditional permission by the South West Africa administration to work in Ovamboland. They were accepted on the condition that they fulfill certain requirements, namely, that they:

1. confine themselves to the area allocated to them
2. conclude their own agreements with the local headmen
3. promise in writing to (a) support and promote government policy, (b) encourage the Ovambo people to work in the south as migrant laborers, (c) teach their members loyalty (tamed) towards the administration, (d) confirm the authority of the headmen and leaders in their territory, and (e) emphasize practical education and only introduce new syllabuses into their schools after discussion with the Director of Bantu Education.[95]

The Anglican School at Odibo was the only one in Ovamboland using English as a medium of instruction. In 1936 it was elevated to the level of Teacher Training Seminary. In 1962 Odibo was developed to the standard of High School. Because of the war, the school was closed in 1979. Two years later its buildings were destroyed by a bomb set by an "unknown" person. The government explained it as "the work of unknown arsonists."

The Anglican Church was probably the first to produce people in leadership positions who were courageous enough to challenge and speak up against black oppression and exploitation. By the mid-1940s the Rev. Michael Scott and the Rev. Theophilus Hamutumbangela of the Anglican clergy were beginning to bring change to Namibian society. Scott lobbied on behalf of the southern Namibian chiefs at the United Nations. Hamutumbangela lobbied the same world body through his letters about the evil system of migratory labor, to which the northern residents in Ovamboland (called simply "Ovambo" by the 1970s) were subjected.

Why did the Anglican Church become conscious of the situation so early on and why were they ready to engage in open conflict with the government? Justin Ellis, one of the people expelled from Namibia because of his stand on violation of human rights, suggests that it was "perhaps because of its connections with the Anglican Church in South Africa [at that time approaching a serious confrontation with the Nationalist Party government]."[96] The South African National Party of the Afrikaaners (Dutch descendants) came to power in 1948 and has never given way since that time.

These two priests, Scott and Hamutumbangela, gave great impetus to the cause which later led to the expulsion of many workers of the Anglican Church. Among those expelled were three successive bishops who openly challenged the oppressive political system: Bishop Robert H. Mize (expelled in 1968) and Bishop Colin O'Brien Winter, who took an uncompromising stand against apartheid (expelled in 1972). Bishop Winter was asked to remain bishop of Damaraland (Namibia) in exile until his death in 1981. Suffragan Bishop Richard Wood was expelled in 1975. Other church workers, including the Rev. Edward Morrow, Justin Ellis, and many others, were also expelled from Namibia.

Although the Namibian Anglican Church has suffered the expulsion of its leaders and workers as well as the destruction of its properties by the South African occupying army, it has decided not to keep silent in the face of social injustice and oppression directed against its members. When the first indigenous bishop of the church,

James Hamupanda Kauluman (who was consecrated on October 10, 1981 and serves as president of the Council of Churches in Namibia) was asked if he had any hope that Namibia would be brought to independence, he expressed the view that whatever happened "we are slaves of hope." Peter Katjavivi, former Secretary of Information for SWAPO, has expressed similar sentiment: "We have come to the end of this road. But we have not lost hope."[97] The Anglican Church, with other churches in the Council of Churches in Namibia, continued to be a voice of the voiceless.

In 1986 Anglican Church membership was over 60,000 in twenty parishes served by thirty priests and many catechists and evangelists. It was also in charge of two schools. Although priests and assistants were trained within Namibia, advanced training was done in South Africa.

The former Diocese of Damarland has become The Anglican Church-Diocese of Namibia. The mission in Ovamboland, with Rev. P. Shilongo as its current archdeacon, is part of the Diocese of Namibia under the leadership of Bishop J. H. Kauluma.

Chronology of Anglican Bishops

N. W. Fogarty	1924–34
C. C. Watts	1934–39
G. W. R. Tobias	1939–49
C. W. Alderson	1949–51
J. D. Vincent	1951–60
R. H. Mize (an American)	1960–68
C. O'Brien Winter	1968–72 (1981)
R. Wood (Suffragan Bishop)	1972–75
J. H. Kauluma (first Namibian)	1981–

THE AFRICAN METHODIST EPISCOPAL CHURCH (AMEC)

The African Methodist Episcopal Church (AMEC) originated outside of Africa. It grew out of the contention between white and Afro-American black Methodists in Philadelphia in the United States of America. The Afro-American blacks decided to form their own church, in which they would not be considered a nuisance in a house of worship or told to go to the back seat while kneeling and praying. These "Africans" of Philadelphia convened together in November 1787 to think seriously about this matter. In 1816 they organized themselves into an independent body. In April 1816 the first General

Conference was held and Richard Allen was elected as the church's first bishop. Among those who laid their hands on Allen at his consecration was Absalom Jones of the Protestant Episcopal Church. "Thus arose the African Methodist Episcopal Church."[99] By 1821 some AMEC missionaries were already in Africa, especially in Sierra Leone and Liberia, although the year 1886 is regarded as the official date for the AMEC's missionary service in Africa.

The origin of the work of the AMEC in southern Africa was connected to the withdrawal, in 1892–95, of a number of African church members of the Wesleyan Missionary Society congregations in South Africa. The seceders formed their own body and adopted the name "Ethiopian Church," based on an interpretation of Psalm 68:31, to the effect that the church in Africa should be governed by Africans themselves. As the color line in the churches of America brought about the AMEC, so the same ill–treatment brought about the "Ethiopian Church" in the churches of Africa.

The "Ethiopian Church" or "Ethiopian Order," with a national vision of the church, was organized at Johannesburg in 1892. Rev. Mangena M. Mokone, a former Wesleyan priest in the Transvaal, was its founder. He wanted equal rights for all within the Methodist organization. Later Mokone was joined by another Wesleyan minister, Dwane. In 1896, at its Pretoria Conference, the church considered the prospect of affiliating with the AMEC in America. To explore the possibility of union, three delegates, including Dwane, were appointed to go the U.S.A. Only Dwane eventually went to America, however.

Early in 1897 Dwane returned under appointment as South African General Superintendent of the African Methodist Episcopal Church. The following year, Bishop Turner of the AMEC visited South Africa at the invitation of the Ethiopian Church. The purpose was to give attention to the Ethiopian concern about the ill–treatment of African Christians by missionary bodies. While the bishop was visiting South Africa, many people were baptized. Many others seceded from societies and joined this church. Sixty ministers and deacons were ordained into the AMEC during the bishop's six week visit.

Before Bishop Turner returned to America he declared the complete union of the Ethiopian Church and the AMEC. Four South Africans of the AMEC were delegated to attend the general conference at Columbus, Ohio in May 1900. South Africa became the Fourteenth Episcopal District, with the Rev. Dr. Levi J. Coppin of Philadelphia as its first resident bishop.

This union did not last long, however. In August 1899 Dwane sought to join the Anglican Church, provided they keep the title "Ethiopian Church" within the Anglican name.[100] In August 1900 Dwane left his position as General Superintendent of the AMEC. He was, then, received into the Anglican Church and appointed Provincial of the Order of Ethiopia.[101] The AMEC was, as a consequence, divided. One section followed Dwane into the Anglican Church; the other remained faithful to its "adopted mother."

Since ill-treatment and prohibitions against black Christians were general phenomena among most missionary societies in Africa, the spirit of the Ethiopian Movement in South Africa soon reached Namibia. The spirit was "fuelled by the rawness of colonial conquest, the resentment caused by settler racism and the struggle over land and labour."[102] The Africans were preaching a doctrine of "Africa for the Africans." This movement aroused the anxiety of colonialists and missionaries, alike.

It was in fact, about 1900 that the Ethiopian Movement was felt in Namibia. *The Missionary Review* of April 1905 reported that the leader of the Nama insurrection, Hendrik Witbooi, was a Christian whom they trusted. But he had been convinced that the Ethiopian Movement leader in that region was a prophet sent by God to free the blacks from white domination. Hendrik had "thrown himself heart and soul into the plans of those who are preaching a black Church for black [people] in Africa."[103]

Although at one point Witbooi was excommunicated from the church, secession did not take place. He was readmitted into the church membership. The Namibian mission work continued to be stable for a long time. But stability does not mean the absence of injustice and discrimination. Black church members continued to be discriminated against by the missionaries. The church leadership remained solely reserved for the missionaries, whereas Africans served at best as evangelists and workers of the missions. Blacks were not allowed to exercise independence. This became the basis of the Ethiopian Movement spirit, which was admired even by the Namibians.

In 1946 a secession of over 8,000 Nama and Damara people took place. They were members of the Rhenish Missionary Society. Markus Witbooi from Gibeon and W. M. Jod from Mariental led the secession. Nama congregations in and around Keetmanshoop and

Malthahöhe also joined the move. They revolted against dependence on the Rhenish Mission and contemplated forming their own independent organization. According to Barret, one of the reasons was that the missionaries interned in the 1940 War asked the Dutch Reformed Church to oversee their Nama churches. The Nama complained about the lack of education for their children.[104] Some of the seceders knew of the AMEC in South Africa.[105] They invited Dr. F. H. Gow, who served as General Superintendent of that church, to come to Namibia. (It seems the AMEC had been working at Lüderitz since 1945 or earlier.)[106] Through Gow these people were received officially into the AMEC. Before this church was allowed to establish itself in Namibia, its work was placed first under the Cape Annual Conference. Bishop Gow is credited with successfully negotiating with the country's administration to get permission to establish the church.

In 1953 a permit was granted and the Cape-South West Africa Annual Conference was held at Keetmanshoop. Bishop Frederick D. Jordan convened the first separate Annual Conference at Windhoek in 1954. The Namibian AMEC is part of the AMEC in South Africa. Namibia is one of the five Annual Conference districts. However, the Namibian district is divided into three sub–districts, each under the presiding elder. In 1972 the districts were: Keetmanshoop under Presiding Elder N. C. Christians, Maltahöhe under Presiding Elder P. A. Schmidt, and Windhoek under Presiding Elder Bartholomeus G. Karuaera.

The AMEC has several schools, including the newly established private school at Gibeon. This school was founded in 1978 and is headed by the Rev. Hendrik Witbooi, who is also Chief of the Nama people and the Vice-President of the South West Africa People's Organization (SWAPO). The African Methodist Episcopal Church is a member of the Council of Churches in Namibia.

THE DUTCH REFORMED CHURCHES

The Dutch Reformed Church is Calvinist in background. It includes: the Dutch Reformed Church in South West Africa, the Reformed Church and the Nederduisch Hervormde Kerk van Afrika. In South Africa it is divided into four different factions, namely, the Dutch Reformed Mission Church (NGSK) for Coloreds, Dutch Reformed Church in Africa (NGKA) for Africans, the Reformed Church in Africa (RCA) for Indians, and the Dutch Reformed Church (DRC) for Whites.

The membership of the Dutch Reformed Churches in Namibia is largely comprised of whites. Its roots in the country can be traced back to the Thirstland Boer Trekkers who came to Namibia from the Transvaal in the 1870s. These Boers belonged mainly to the Dutch Reformed Church. Because of the British pressure, under Commissioner W. C. Palgrave, the Trekkers trekked to Angola, where they established Dutch Reformed Church congregations. Some Boers did not go to Angola, but remained behind at Grootfontein. Those who remained behind were ministered to by the Dutch Reformed Church ministers from South Africa as one of their outstations. However, the first DRC congregation in Namibia was established at Warmbad in 1898. Other congregations were founded at Gibeon and Grootfontein, but there was a problem with obtaining legal status for them from the German authorities. At the time of the 1919 Mandate, these congregations were legalized and were allowed to join the Cape Synod.

In 1928 the Angola Boers were repatriated to Namibia by the Union administration of the country. They settled in Gobabis, Aranos, and Leonardville. More DRC congregations were established at these places. South Africa's occupation of the country since 1915, also contributed to the increase of DRC membership, new members arriving from the Union of South Africa in connection with the occupation.

More congregations and a larger membership made it necessary to establish an independent synod of South West Africa, affiliated with the five synods of South Africa. The synod was formed on May 5, 1957. The church has purportedly received government aid. It maintains chaplains and social workers, secretariats for missions, poor-relief, and evangelization programs. It also has three nursing homes, a crèche, and an orphanage.[107]

Although the Reformed faith was introduced into Namibia in the nineteenth century, the Boers did not do mission work. Only their servants could learn their faith from them. On this basis, the Angola Boers trekked back to Namibia; some of the Angolan people were converted to the Reformed faith. These Christians were known as "tamed people" of Angola. Formal mission work, nevertheless, was not practiced by the DRC.

By 1910, however, those blacks who were servants to the Boers or who were living near established Dutch Reformed congregations could listen to the regular preaching. At this time there were a number of Dutch Reformed ministers, like E. J. Leonard, who attempted regular preaching to the Africans. Such efforts developed into a sense of extending the Christian mission to the Africans. It was not, however, until September 1, 1962 that the first synod of the Dutch Reformed Mission Church was held. The same year new congregations were established at Karasburg, Rehoboth, Gobabis, and Walvis Bay.

In the early 1950s some Dutch Reformed ministers travelled to Kaokoveld to preach. Later missionaries who were sent there included a minister, a nurse and an evangelist. A "non-white" Dutch Reformed Mission School at Orumana, in Kaokoveld, has been providing theological training to African Reformed students. Before the school was established, the students and church workers received their education at Stoffberg Theological School, Umtata, Paulinum, and at Dorothea Mission in Pretoria. The Dutch Reformed Church extended its mission to Tsumkwe among the San, Okavango, and Owambo as well, even moreso after the 1960s when the Mission Church was founded. The mission to the Ovambo is the most recent one. In 1973 a Dutch Reformed congregation was founded at Onumo in Uukwanyama (Oukwanyama). Other congregations have also been established. In July 1975 the Dutch Reformed Mission Church was re-named the "Evangelical Reformed Church in Africa." Its membership is concentrated in Owambo, Okavango, and Kaoko. Its leadership is mostly white. And it has observer status in the Council of Churches in Namibia.

THE METHODIST CHURCH OF SOUTHERN AFRICA

Reference has already been made to the fact that in 1867 the Wesleyan Methodist mission stations were taken over by the Rhenish Mission.[108] This was, it seems, only a temporary situation, lasting only until another opportunity was opened up.

Joseph Wood, the first Wesleyan minister to the Namibian whites wrote in a letter of 1920 that some black Methodists came to Lüderitz from the Cape Colony. There, they had from 1908–1910 begun to build their church. In Windhoek, Methodist services had been held since 1916. The evangelist Alfred Mralasi from the Transkei came to minister in 1919. In due course, the Rehoboth Basters were served by visiting Methodist ministers between the years 1920 and 1923. J. R. Pieterse and F. Scheepers were two of these ministers.

As time passed more churches and schools were erected in various places, including Rehoboth and Kalkrand.[109] In 1984 Rev. Alan Brews was the head of the Methodist Church of Southern Africa in Namibia.

THE APOSTOLIC FAITH MISSION

The Apostolic Faith Mission was organized at Maltahöhe in 1940 among the white people. It was later extended to Windhoek, Grootfontein and other places as far away as Owambo, with its center near Ondangwa where, in 1917, it claimed 1,800 to 2,000 members (cf. Kritzinger).[110]

THE SEVENTH DAY ADVENTISTS

The Seventh Day Adventists have been working in East Caprivi since 1921. They have a large following in the country. About 300 members of the Seventh Day Adventist faith were reported by Tötemeyer at Oshakati, Owambo in 1972.[111]

OTHER DENOMINATIONS AND MOVEMENTS

The following religious denominations have also been reported to have established a presence in Namibia. We shall only mention them briefly without giving any details. Some might have more impact on the Namibian people than those described above; however, examination and detailed accounts were not based on any preference. Some of the listed denominations or movements could be of great interest if their history was detailed, for example, the "Oruuano."

1. Baha'i Church
2. Baptist Church, headed by the Rev. Kandume at Oshakati
3. Christian Brethren
4. Ovambo Independent Church, headed by Peter Kalangula at Ondangwa
5. Kimbanguist (probably came to Namibia through people from Angola)
6. The Full Gospel of Jesus; came to Namibia about 1955
7. The Full Evangelical Church of Christ; mostly in Okavango at Kapuku, also in Owambo (Ovamboland)
8. Zionists from South Africa
9. Southern Baptist Convention (recent, from the USA)
10. Church of God (Cleveland) (recent, from the USA)
11. "Oruuano" (Community or the Herero Church, ex-Rhenish Mission). Oruuano seceded in 1955 and further split into four factions: (1) Church of Africa; (2) The African Church; (3) Protestant Unity Church; (4) The Herero Church[112]
12. Rhenish (Basters) Congregation, former Rhenish Mission faction of Rehoboth Basters who refused to join the new Lutheran

Church, ELCSWA, at the time of its establishment in 1962 for fear of losing its rights as a "Coloured" community within the "Bantu" church according to the apartheid laws ingrained in the people. By that time "Coloured" had rights of estate but not "Bantu"

13. Watch-Tower, in Caprivi

14. United Congregational Church of Southern Africa-Gordonia Region. It is connected to South Africa and has been in the country since about 1950 among the Colored/Basters. Congregational Church congregations are to be found in Windhoek, where Pastor Peter Lamoela was its first pastor, Walvis Bay, Rehoboth, Kalkfeld, and Lüderitz

15. St. Philip's Healing Church

16. St. John Apostolic Faith Mission

17. South Africa General Mission (SAGM-D.R.C.). It has been in Rundu, Okavango since 1971

18. Independent Rhenish Mission of South Africa (ex-Rhenish Mission) in Rehoboth; came into being about 1959 (see number 12 above)

19. The Dorothea Mission with its headquarters in Pretoria. It came to Namibia in 1947 through Hannes Joubert. In 1952 this Mission conducted a major revival ("Epapudhuko") in Ovamboland. Dorothea Mission is not a church, and it is probably not a movement aiming to be an independent church *per se;* therefore, its representatives belong to different churches in the country, including Lutheran churches[113]

20. Baptist Union of South Africa, mostly in Walvis Bay and Windhoek among the whites. Its headquarters are in Johannesburg

21. Salvation Army; came to Namibia about the 1930s

22. Church of the Latter Reign (or Blourokkies), a Pentecostal branch among the Afrikaners

23. Presbyterian Church of Southern Africa, mostly whites

24. Jehovah's Witnesses; came in about 1945

25. Christian Assemblies among the Colored/Basters; probably came to Namibia about 1950

26. Independent Rhenish Mission of South Africa at Rehoboth

27. Church of Jesus Christ of the Latter-day Saints, a branch of the Mormons from the U.S.A.

28. New Apostolic, an ex-Catholic Church from Germany; came about 1910. It is found among the German immigrants

29. Full Gospel Church of God in Southern Africa

30. Apostolic Spiritual Healing Church from Botswana, mostly among the Tswana people

31. Spiritual Healing Church, another healing movement with links to Botswana and Lesotho

32. Free Gospel Church

It is possible that many more religious bodies may have existed in Namibia. Statistics of membership of each of these denominations and movements were not available during the course of this research.[114]

NOTES

1. Theodore Huggenvik, *An Outline of Church History* (Minneapolis: Augsburg Publishing House, 1939), 264, citing G. P. Fisher, "History of the Christian Church," Ch. 9.

2. *Ibid.*

3. C. P. Groves, *The Planting of Christianity in Africa,* Vol. 1 (London, 1948), 125.

4. *Ibid.,* 138.

5. Jane M. Sales, *The Planting of the Churches in South Africa* (Michigan: Wm. B. Eerdman's Publishing Co., 1971), 16–17.

6. Edwin Munsell Bliss, *The Encyclopedia of Missions* (New York: Funk & Wagnalls, 1891), I:555.

7. Robert Moffat, *Missionary Labors and Scenes in Southern Africa* (New York: Robert Carter & Bros., 1842), 78.

8. The Afrikaner family was outlawed in the Cape Colony. They then fled to Namibia in the nineteenth century.

9. Moffat, 173–79. See also Groves, 1:240–41.

10. Elfriede Strassberger, *The Rhenish Mission Society in South Africa* (Cape Town: C. Struik (Pty) Ltd., 1969), 67.

11. *Ibid.*

12. John O. Choules and Thomas Smith, *The Origin of Missions,* Vol. 2 (Boston: Crocker & Brewster, 1837), 1.

13. J. Du Plessis, *A History of Christian Missions in South Africa* (Cape Town: C. Struik, 1965), 167.

14. Choules and Smith, 2:153.

15. *Ibid.,* 155.

16. William Ragsdale Cannon, *History of Christianity in the Middle Ages* (Michigan: Baker Book House, 1960), 89.

17. Du Plessis, 201.

18. Elsie Singmaster, *The Story of Lutheran Missions* (Columbia: Press of Survey Publishing Co., 1917), 130.

19. George Drach, *Our Church Abroad* (Philadelphia: The United Lutheran Publishing House, 1926), 215.

20. Michael Deets, *Lutheran World Information: 1/87* (Geneva: LWF, 1987), 3.

21. Du Plessis, 117.

22. *Ibid.*, 206.
23. Julius Baumann, *Van Sending tot Kerk* (Karibib, 1967), 31.
24. Canon, 89.
25. Horst Drechsler, *Let Us Die Fighting* (Zed Press, 1980), 114.
26. *To Be Born a Nation* (Zed Press, 1981), 12.
27. Shituwa (+ 13.1.1969) takes charge in the west, Kafita in the east. Meanwhile, an English official called Mr. Fairlie assisted these Christians in building a church at Omafo, not far east of Engela. Liljeblad of the F.M.S. baptized 55 adults and many children at Omafo in 1918. When Engela was founded by August Hanninen from Oshigambo in 1921, many of these Christians at Omafo became members of the new congregation at Engela. Therefore, the membership of Engela was about 4,000 in 1923 and 8,427 in 1986. See also Natanael Shinana, "Ondjokomona yomufita Ismael-Abraham yaThomas Nhinda", in *Omukwetu* (Oniipa, June 30, 1986), p. 9. In 1903 the Rhenish Mission in Ovamboland had 3 stations, 5 missionaries, 2 African workers, 35 communicants and 130 pupils.
28. *CWM, Agenda, Field Report, Germany* (LWF, 1956), 13.
29. *Ibid.* (1960), 17.
30. Thomas M. J. Leeuw, "The Church in Southern Africa" in *The Church in Africa: 1977*, ed. Charles R. Taber (California: William Carey Library, 1977), 45.
31. *Ibid.*
32. *Ibid.*, 44.
33. Carl-J. Hellberg, *A Voice of the Voiceless* (Lund: Verbum, 1979), 148.
34. *Ibid.* 149.
35. "Statement on Southern Africa: Confessional Integrity" (LWF, August 1, 1984), Articles 2-4.
36. Edwin Munsell Bliss, *The Encyclopedia of Missions*, 1:371.
37. J. N. Lenker, *Lutherans in All Lands* (Milwaukee: Lutherans in All Lands Co., 1896), 414.
38. *Ibid.*
39. Bliss, 372.
40. Burton L. Goddard, *The Encyclopedia of Modern Christian Missions* (New Jersey: Thomas Nelson & Sons, 1967), 620.
41. It is easy to confuse this Carl Hugo Hahn with his sons, viz., Carl Hugo Hahn Jr., Hugo Hahn and Traugott Hahn. All were pastors. There were also other Hahns who worked in Namibia or South Africa or both, such as Johannes Samuel Hahn, the father of Johannes Hahn, Johannes Theophilus Hahn and Paul Daniel Hahn.
42. Bliss, 372.
43. *Ibid.*
44. Toivo E. Tirronen, *Nakambalekanene* (Oniipa: ELCIN Press, 1977), 12.
45. According to Tirronen, it was at 1:23 a.m. and that would make the arrival date January 1, 1869. See Tirronen, 20.
46. Lenker, 417.
47. *Ibid.*, 416. "Malmström and Jurwelin first presented themselves, were accepted and sent to the Hermannsburg mission school in Germany for preparation. The former was appointed in 1866 to the Hermannsburg station, Matlabe in Bechuanaland, South Africa, and the latter remained to learn German until 1868, when he was ordained in Hermannsburg. . . . Malmström and Jurwelin . . . transferred their relations and the Ovambo station started with ten laborers."
48. Tirronen, 20.
49. See note 47 above.
50. This mission station lasted only for a few weeks or months before it was given up. The missionaries were expelled from Uukwambi by King Nuuyoma in May 1872.

51. Bliss, 373.

52. *Oshipala shaELOK* (Oniipa: ELCIN Press, 1978), 28.

53. "Die Geskiedenis van die Evangeliese Lutherse Ovambokavangokerk" (Oniipa: ELCIN Archives, undated), 3–4.

54. The membership of the ELCIN, given to the LWF as 349,816 the same year, does not correspond with the number from the congregations, which totalled 350,266.

55. Cf. Tirronen, 67.

56. H. O. Dwight, *The Encyclopedia of Missions* (New York: Funk & Wagnalls, 1904), 237.

57. *International Review of Missions* (New York, 1937), 76.

58. *Oshipala shaELOK,* 57; and Erkki Laurmaa, *Afrika jUuningininomutenja* (Helsinki, 1949), 123. Evangelists were trained at Oniipa and Engela. Some were given the task of preaching and teaching schools without much required formal education from the state. But "Oya talwa aadhiginini, ye shi ku uvitha nokupukulula ooyakwawo, onkee ya pewa oshilonga shika. Oyendji yaambaka oyo aalongi yoosikola."

59. Heikki Ausiku and Taimi Saari, *Histoli zosirugana sEtumo moKavango*. See also *Omukwetu* (Oniipa, May 15, 1986), 6.

60. *Omukwetu*)Oniipa, May 15, 1986), 1, 4, 7. Their teacher was Ruben Kandjumbu.

61. The father of Teddy Aarni, the author of *The Kalunga Concept in Ovambo Religion from 1870 Onwards* (Stockholm, 1982).

62. *Oshipala shaELOK,* 55.

63. Groves, 4:243.

64. *Omukwetu* (May 15, 1986), 1, 9; and *Omukwetu* (July 15, 1986), 6–7.

65. *Oshipala shaELOK,* 56.

66. It is known as the Evangelical Lutheran Church in SWA (Rhenish Mission) because since the blacks do not hold rights to property by law, the church's properties still legally belong to the Rhenish Mission. This will remain the case until such laws are scrapped. Today there are some changes which may be used by the church in order to own those properties itself.

67. Huggenvik, 90.

68. Du Plessis, 368.

69. Leeuw, 48–49.

70. W. E. Brown, *The Catholic Church in South Africa* (New York, 1960), 139.

71. *Ibid.*

72. Bernard Huss, "The Roman Catholic Church" in *Christianity and the Natives,* ed. J. Dexter Taylor, 305.

73. It was established to serve the needs of the European colonists and was divided into: the Vicariate Apostolic of Western Cape Colony (1837); the Vicariate of Central Cape Colony (1874); and that of Eastern Cape Colony (1847). The Orange River Prefecture, established by the Holy Ghost Fathers, was later made over to the Oblates of St. Francis de Sales at Troyes. It was raised to a vicariate in 1898. See Charles G. Herbermann, ed., *The Catholic Encyclopedia,* Vol. 1 (New York: The Encyclopedia, Inc., 1913), 188–89.

74. The Vicariate Apostolic of the Two Guineas (1841) "extended from Senegal to the Orange River, with the exception of the region, then hardly occupied, included in the Portuguese Diocese of St. Paul de Loanda. This vast country was gradually partitioned out, and there arose the present system of missions, prefectures and vicariate apostolic. . . ." Herbermann, 189.

75. Brown, 140.

76. "The Portuguese Bishopric of Angola and Congo had been maintained at Loanda, but the Portuguese missions, properly so called, had entirely disappeared,

when the daring initiative of Father Duparquet, of the Holy Ghost, undertook their revival. In 1872 he founded a permanent post at Landana, which has become the head-quarters of the Lower Congo, or Portuguese Congo, Mission. In 1881, the mission of the Huilla Plateau was started, which was to extend its sphere of action beyond the Cunene; in 1884, the Prefecture Apostolic of Cimbebasia included Cassinga, then Ca-conda, Bihe, Massaca, and Cuanyama, and reached almost as far as the basin of the Upper Zambezi." Herbermann, 189. See also *New Catholic Encyclopedia*, Vol. 13, (New York: The Catholic University of America, Washington D.C., 1967), 485–86.

77. G. B. A. Gardener, *Recent Developments in the South African Mission Field* (Cape Town: N. G. Kerk Uitgewers, 1958), 123. *Standard Encyclopedia of Southern Africa*, Vol. 10 (SLE-TUN, Nasau, Ltd., 1974), 189.

78. According to Du Plessis, the whole of Namibia, except the most southerly por-tion, forms a prefecture of Cimbebasia Inferior. Du Plessis, 368. See also note 76 above.

79. Brown, 142.

80. Three patres, Duparquet, Hogan and Griffin, attempted to settle in 1878 but the opposition of Chaherani, Chief of Omaruru, compelled them to beat a retreat. The attempt to found a Catholic mission among the Herero was not renewed until 1896, when the Oblates of Mary Immaculate entered the mission field. Governor Leutwein stipulated that they should keep at a due distance from Rhenish Missions. These fathers were ejected from Omaruru by force in 1881 with a consequent outcry at Herero bar-barity and Protestant intolerance. Du Plessis, 368; and Groves, 2:250–51.

81. Brown, 142.

82. *Ibid.*, 143.

83. *Ibid.*, 149.

84. "On 10 January 1921 it became simply the Cimbebasia Prefecture, the Portu-guese having relinquished that style; and on 11 May 1926 it became the Windhoek Vi-cariate. It surrendered that part of its territory which extended into Bechuanaland when the new prefecture of Bechuanaland was created in the spring of 1959." Brown, 337.

85. *Ibid.*, p. 150. This vicariate was originally part of the old Prefecture of Cimbe-basia, in Angola. It was made into the Lower (Inferior) Cimbebasia Prefecture on Au-gust 1, 1892.

86. *Ibid.*, 151.

87. "In 1879 the Jesuits came to [Olukonda], and the king gave them permission to stay, but they went farther north . . .in 1882 they over-reached the borders of the mis-sion, but the natives drove them away." Bliss, 373.

88. Gerdener, 123.

89. *Omukuni* (Windhoek, August 1974), 3.

90. Laurmaa, 102.

91. *Standard Encyclopedia of Southern Africa*, 10:190.

92. Laurmaa, 97.

93. *Ibid.*

94. *Ibid.*, 100.

95. Gerhard Tötemeyer, *Namibia, Old and New* (London: C. Hurst, 1978), 23.

96. Justin Ellis, "The Church in Mobilization for National Liberation" in *Namibia: The Last Colony*, ed. Reginald H. Green et. al. (Longman, 1981), 134.

97. Ed May, *Namibia: Update* (New York: USA National Committee of L. W. In-formation, Feburary 6, 1981).

98. Bishop Kauluma was born in the northern region of Namibia (Owambo) and grew up looking after his father's cattle. His father was not a Christian and had many

Namibian Churches Under Colonialism

III

THE MISSION OF THE CHURCH in Namibia has been affected by several factors, including severe droughts and famines, diseases and deaths of missionaries and church workers, expulsions and exilings of priests and church members, and the World Wars. Above all, colonialism, apartheid, and the migratory labor system are the worst factors—and these could be avoided. The latter three will be considered in these few pages. The explosive nature of this history will be analysed from the ideological, colonial, imperialistic, and possibly capitalistic points of view which we shall examine here.

Mission and Colonialism

Christian *mission* is taken to mean the proclamation of the gospel to the unconverted everywhere according to the command of Christ with directives of *making disciples, baptizing,* and *teaching* to observe all things commanded by Jesus.[1]

The term "colonialism," on the other hand,

appears to be a recent arrival in the languages of the western world, taking the place of the older and more familiar "imperialism." It is used almost exclusively as a term of reproach, implying that the only aim of colonial rule has been the exploitation and impoverishment of weak and defenceless peoples, and that its only results have been the destruction of what was good in ancient civilizations and the multiplication of measureless evils.[2]

Christian missionaries entered Namibia over eighty years before the territory was subjugated under colonial rule. The missionary enterprise was a matter of fighting darkness with light, evil with good, heathenism and/or paganism with Christianity. Sometimes it was to convert both heathens and Protestants or to evangelize the "darkened hearts" and "lost souls" of the Africans. There were many aims and goals of the several missionary activities. However, the good intentions of even those who came to Namibia cannot be denied. Many good things have happened in their name and mission. In following the call to spread the gospel, they suffered separation from their relatives and those whom they knew. They exposed themselves to many dangers both on sea and land. They took pains to learn new languages. No short or simple summary of the place and effects of missionaries in Namibia can give an adequate or complete picture of their place in the history of the region.

The most unfortunate thing about even the best missionaries is that most of them never took the pains to relinquish their European conceptions of all Africans as godless and savages. They failed to see that the people of Africa were religious and had a sincere reverence of worship. Neither was civilization introduced by the European missionaries or colonists. Africa had its own civilization before they came. The Europeans did not learn these truths:

The real Africa was very different from the Africa described by the slave trader. For one thing, it could no more be spoken of as one unified continent than Europe could. Africa was a land of many languages, religions, colors, and stages of development. In the years before the arrival of the Europeans, Africa achieved a cultural progress equal to and often superior to that of Europe. During the African metal age that began 500 years before the birth of Christ, the African people began to cultivate the soil, build great cities, develop their arts, smelt and work iron ore, and build complex social systems. African craftsmen were skilled in leather, wood, glass, gold, ivory, copper, tin, silver and bronze.[3]

The Europeans felt free to treat the Africans in any way they pleased simply because "Africans were not Christians." They claimed to offer both Christianity and civilization to the Africans in place of "African savagery."[4]

The story of the relationship of mission and colonialism in Namibia is a long one. It begins with German missionaries of the Rhenish Mission Society (RMS), which established itself in the country in 1842. The arrival of other Germans is related to crucial events in the German homeland. It is also worth noting that the connection among mission, politics, and colonial occupation of Namibia was very close.[5]

It was not until the 1800s that Germany was to unite herself, under the leadership of King William I and Prince Otto Edwin Leopold von Bismarck. The economic and political revolution of Germany took place in the 1850s and 1860s.[6] The unification and establishment of the German Empire in 1870 enabled Germany to embark on industrialization and take an interest in the European scramble for and partition of Africa. Meanwhile, we have to note that:

In 1879 more than 90 percent of the continent was ruled by Africans. By 1900 all but a tiny fraction of it was being governed by European powers. By about 1914 the lives of almost all Africans were being deeply affected by the changes brought about by these foreign rulers. The European powers partitioned Africa among themselves with such haste, like players in a rough game, that the process has been called "the scramble for Africa."[7]

In 1939 the whole of Africa was controlled by the Europeans. Ethiopia was occupied by Italy, Egypt was in the hands of British troops in the Suez Canal Zone, and the American Firestone Rubber Company practically dominated the country of Liberia. Although the Union of South Africa was within the Commonwealth of Britain, the blacks were dominated by the minority white population. The whole of Africa could be said to be under "firmly rooted" European rule.[8] Germany came late into the "scramble for Africa" and the "colonial market." This lateness was an outgrowth of Bismarck's initial unwillingness to take an active interest in the colonial question. However, groups and individuals in Germany demanded colonies, their demands grew more powerful, and Bismarck suddenly changed his attitude. Between 1883 and 1885 European diplomats were caught by surprise when Bismarck declared Togo, Cameroun, Tanzania, and Namibia to be German protectorates. The Berlin Conference of 1884–85 opened a way for Bismarck to proceed with his plan of acquiring some parts of Africa.[9]

The German missionaries played a role in the acquisition of Namibia. Their conduct was one of the classic examples of how Christian missionary societies could paralyze countries' "natural powers of defence and . . . pave the way for colonial subjugation."[10] Early in 1864 the Prussian flag flew over the mission colony building at Otjimbingwe. In 1868 Hugo Hahn, on behalf of the missionaries and especially for himself, requested protection from the Prussian government. This was partly because of the plundering of mission properties by the Namibians at Scheppmannsdorf and Otjimbingwe. Since Germany was neither united nor yet interested in colonies, the German Empire referred the missionaries' appeal to the British government in the Cape. This whole affair of referral led to the eventual protectorate declaration over the territory and the annexation of Walvis Bay by the Cape Colony authority on behalf of Britain in 1878. This in itself was step one in the process of colonization. Commissioner W. C. Palgrave was sent from the Cape Colony to fulfill this task of annexation by signing treaties with the local indigenous leaders; their lack of information about what was really at stake and the long range goals involved would have effects on the region which are still being felt. They were purposely kept unaware of the actual implications of such treaties. The idea of a treaty was received positively by Chief Maharero of the Herero and was rejected by the Nama. For the missionaries it was better to enjoy British protection if German protection was unavailable or denied. Therefore, they rejoiced on the coming of the British.

A Rhenish missionary, C. G. Büttner, who zealously promoted the German colonial authority in Namibia, was in line with the then Director of the Rhenish Missionary Society, Mr. F. Fabri, who was the society's director for more than twenty-five years, beginning in 1857. Fabri "had seen the 'usefulness' of the mission 'for the trade that might follow, or colonial annexation.' "[11] "The Missions-Handels-Aktiengesellschaft" was founded in 1870 as a trading company. It also "specialized in the import of weapons and ammunition"[12] to Namibia, but it became ineffective because there was no other way to import weapons into Namibia with Britain in Walvis Bay. This, again, prompted the missionaries to request German protection or occupation of the territory, if necessary.

In his often-quoted letter of June 3, 1880 to the German Foreign Office, Fabri explained the reason that the society opted for British protection: "Therefore, the Society's Executive respected the English occupation, despite the burdens it entailed, as a fact that was, on the whole, conducive to the common weal of the country and to its development."[13]

Friedrich Fabri is also known as one of the great champions of German colonial expansion. In 1879 he published a book with the interesting title *Does Germany Need Colonies? (Bedarf Deutschland der Kolonien?)*. His answer to his question was affirmative. His argument was grounded in the notion that since Germans had already emigrated to other colonies in the world and become subjects of foreign powers, and since it seemed impossible to stop emigration, it was, therefore, necessary

that Germany herself should find colonies somewhere in the temperate zones, and populate them with those for whom there was no room at home. . . . Fabri also uses the fallacious argument of trade with such colonies . . . suggesting that Christian missions can be useful for the purposes of colonization.[14]

In 1882 Fabri became chairman of the German Colonial Society. His ideas were becoming a reality. The following year Lüderitz, a German trader from Bremen, occupied an area around Angra Pequena in November and signed treaties with the Namibian chiefs. On April 24, 1884 the German Consul at the Cape informed the South African authorities that the Angra Pequena area was now under German protection. On August 7 it was clear to almost everybody that Namibia had become a German colony. The German missionaries were thrilled at this occupation.

The government tended to build its stations and places of residence precisely at those centres which had already been developed as mission stations. Inevitably the Africans began to think that the missionaries were in alliance with the government and with the German settlers, who were coming in increasing numbers and gradually taking over much of the best land in the country.[15]

When the missionaries at Otjimbingwe sold one of their buildings to the government, they also sold the land upon which the building was standing. This action was a violation of Namibian traditional laws. Customarily, in the Namibian laws of the land, one can occupy a portion of land, but one cannot be allowed to possess it. The land belongs to all people; it cannot be bought. This transaction of the land between the missionaries and the new government put the Namibians in so hostile a position towards the missionaries that one of the Herero chiefs ordered the church at Okiahandja to be closed. However, this order was never carried out and it was soon withdrawn.[16]

We have looked into what can be termed a positive collaboration between missionaries and colonial governments. However, we should also note that in later years missionaries were disappointed by colonial rule and, therefore, lost their "initial enthusiasm."

[In Namibia] it was a German mission that carried the most total responsibility. . . . The Rhenish missionaries, as patriotic Germans, naturally welcomed the setting up of the German protectorate. But they also saw in it an extension of their missionary opportunity. . . . But in the issue these happy anticipations were far from being realised, as twenty years later they were compelled to admit. Some, it is true, expressed misgivings at the time, counseling caution in relations with the government in case matters went awry, but such warnings were rejected as unpatriotic.[17]

The mission of the church was negatively affected by this collaboration with the government. Although the missionaries, Büttner among others, were involved in concluding treaties between colonial rulers and local chiefs, the Namibians were never fully informed that they were now German subjects. In 1886, within two months after they had learned that, the Nama chiefs concluded peace treaties with the Herero chiefs. Although the two, Herero and Nama, were former foes who fought seven years of "heavy" warfare between 1863 and 1870 and warred again in 1880, they found themselves standing on common ground in their mutual desire to fight back and resist the colonial powers. In 1888 chief and church elder Hendrick Witbooi of the Nama wrote a letter to the Herero chief Maharero, who seemed to be much in favor of the German "protection," saying:

You call yourself Supreme Chief of Damaraland [Gererikabd] . . . but my dear Kaptein you have now accepted another earthly government, the German government, in order to protect yourself from the terrors of our war power and through this mighty nation to destroy me. . . . My dear Kaptein, you will eternally regret your action in having handed over to the white man the right to govern your country. After all, our war is not as serious a matter as you think . . . but this thing that you have done, that you are doing, to surrender yourself to the white man, will be a burden that you will carry on your shoulders (as if you were carrying the sun on your back). You will not understand Göring's actions and you will in due course resent them, and then it will be too late for you, seeing that you will already have given them the unqualified right of control. He will not yield to your wishes and you will not wish to yield to his, but then it will be too late.[18]

In 1904, only about sixteen years after his prophetic letter to the Herero chief, Witbooi was convinced that the leader of the "Ethiopian Movement" who visited him was "a prophet sent from God to free the blacks from white domination, and he has thrown himself heart and soul into the plans of those who are preaching a black Church for black men [people] in Africa."[19] At this time Witbooi was finding ways to strengthen himself before he embarked on public revolt against the white domination. On October 3, 1904 he wrote to a Rhenish "missionary," Mr. Holzapfel, at Rietmond, asking him to surrender all the ammunition (cartridges and powder) on the reservation farm to him (Witbooi), because he had "broken with the German government." Mr. Holzapfel refused and hid the arms instead. Witbooi commanded his cadres to execute Holzapfel. Holzapfel tried to flee by ox wagon, but he was "finished" near Mariental.

In fact, this was Witbooi's first action in joining the Herero in their national resistance against the German presence. This war of resistance was waged between 1903 and 1907. This dramatic war, with German forces under the command of the notorious German human extermination specialist General Von Trotha, ended with the reduction of the Herero nation from 80,000 to 20,000, and the Nama nation from 20,000 to 9,700. "No fewer than 80 percent of the Herero and 50 percent of the Nama had thus fallen victim to German colonial rule."[20] Germans, who had reinforced their troops to 14,000, were reported to have "lost 2,000 men and were forced to spend $120 million to re-establish their authority."[21]

Before the subjugation and maiming of the Namibians by the Germans' heavy artillery, missionaries could claim only a small number of converts, or none, in some parts of the country. It took thirteen years in Ovamboland and about twenty years in Hereroland (Damarland) before the first baptisms took place. As soon as the period of Namibian massacres and other national calamaties was over, missionaries reported a considerable growth in the number of Christians in their mission fields. Here lay the danger of superficial Christianity for the church in Namibia: There were many in number but how many in spirit? However, the reports were like this one of 1915–16:

The Protestant missions are the German Rhenish Mission with 47 men, 6 single women and a Christian community of 26,000 and the Finnish Missionary Society with 9 stations and about 3,000 Christians. The Roman Catholic missions are those of the Oblates of the Immaculate Virgin Mary (Hunfeld) in the north with 23 priests, 25 lay brothers, 22 sisters and about 1,000 Christians, and of the Austrian Salesians of Troyes in Great Namaqualand with 8 priests, 9 sisters and about 1,500 Christians. The latest reports seem to indicate that the Rhenish missionaries have been allowed to return to the southern stations.[22]

And Groves says:

The Protestant missioniaries demoralize the natives by training them to sing and pray (at which 75 per cent are hypocrites) instead of work; and preaching to them on their universal human rights instead of inculcating their duties.[23]

Even if the quotation from Groves cannot be the whole truth, there is some truth in it considering the mass baptisms soon after the war. This was not something unique to Namibia. Elsewhere in the history of religions, it is true that subjects were usually forced to follow the rulers' religion and beliefs. The example of Emperor Constantine serves as a classic case in this regard. However, much of the growth in numbers of Christians among indigenous Namibians has been attributed to German pride and success in crushing the Namibians. It was this which prompted Dr. Gustav Warneck to say:

It has been a laborious work of patience that the missionaries have done in these great countries, industrially so poor—a work made difficult by the great inconstancy of the Hottentots and the Herero, as well as by the entanglements of war,—and more than once in Hereroland the workers were on a point of withdrawing. But German fidelity at last carried the day. Now the whole of the great region from the Orange River to beyond Walfisch Bay, far into the interior of Great Nama land and Herero land and even up to Ovambo land is covered with a network of stations. All the points that could be occupied have been made mission stations and the whole population has been brought under the educative and civilizing influence of Christianity.[24]

The mission of the church suffered in the colonial expansion and during the ensuing wars. After World War I there was a shift in mission/colonial relationships. South Africa invaded Namibia in 1914–15 under British orders with over 40,000 troops. The German garrison of 8,000 could not defend themselves. They surrendered to the South African forces under General Louis Botha at Khorab on July 9, 1915.

The Rhenish missionaries were to leave most of their former stations, especially in the northern part of the country.

With the advance of the Union troops a number were temporarily taken prisoner. Some of whom were sent to the Union while others were held in South West Africa. They were soon released and permitted to resume their missionary activity.[25]

According to the *International Review*, it was reported that:

Information with regard to the fate of the missionaries is not available, except that those in the southern stations of the Rhenish Society were in the course of the hostilities removed to Natal (South Africa) and subsequently set at liberty, though not allowed to return to their field. The Finnish missionaries in Ovamboland were for nearly a year cut off from the outside world, and their supply of provisions barely sufficed to support them.[26]

Already at the beginning of the war there was confrontation in Rehoboth between the Basters and the missionaries. The Basters perceived the missionaries to be in support of the German soldiers, while they favored the South African troops. Although the Basters were forced to conscript into the German army, they did not want to shoot at the South Africans, because they themselves had come from South Africa to Namibia. One of the Basters' leaders asked

South African General Botha if they could be of help to him. The offer was rejected on the grounds that the war was "a war of Whites against Whites . . . and did not concern the Rehobothers."[27] The real reason was that since the whites were "superior" and the Basters and others were "inferior," no "superior" could allow another "superior" to be killed by an "inferior"—even if they were enemies. Because of the seemingly close alliance of the Basters to the South Africans, they refused to be under a Rhenish missionary and preferred a missionary from South Africa. Therefore, some Dutch Reformed Church missionaries worked among the Basters for a short period until peace was again established with the former missionaries. In this way the Dutch Reformed Church was able to pave the way for its future mission in the territory.

In the wake of the war, German missionaries were not totally expelled from Namibia, although they had financial problems because all resources from Germany were cut off. Both Protestant and Catholic missionaries experienced the same problem of lack of funds. The work of the missionaries was thus crippled by the war. This was most true with the German missionaries. The Finnish missionaries in Ovamboland were able to continue unhindered and even took over the former Rhenish stations in that region, despite the fact that they, too, had been cut off from the outside world for almost a year.

The post-World War I period in Namibia brought with it a number of issues. The arrival of the English soldiers made it possible for the Anglican Church to come into Namibia. English pastors came in as chaplains to the soldiers and later extended their work to evangelize the indigenous peoples. It was from the Anglican Church that most of the later pioneers in public denouncement of colonialism and the apartheid policy came. The Rev. Michael Scott was one such pioneer.

On the other hand, the Rhenish missionaries were criticized and labelled as participants in the subjugation of the Namibian population. The criticisms were based on their writings and conduct. The criticisms had already started at the beginning of the German takeover of the territory. These missionaries generally seemed to show no sympathy to the conquered blacks in the war of mass extermination of the Herero, Damara and Nama and the enslavement of those who survived the genocide. In the words of Praeses Dr. H. Vedder of the Rhenish Mission, who had worked in Namibia since 1903:

The Herero have yet to realize that there are other nationalities with rights in South West Africa besides themselves who have a right to existence. But if the Herero haughtily decline the opportunities offered them for developing and working themselves up and persist in wishing to live an isolated life, according to their own ideas, there are distinct signs that brutalization, degeneration, childlessness, rapidly increasing sexual diseases, bodily debilitation, in consequence of spirituous native drinks, will end in their digging their own national grave.[28]

The cooperation of the missionaries and the German colonial government was also felt abroad in their endeavors to neutralize the indigenous people who attempted to be independent instead of submitting to their new "masters."

In German South West Africa, where there would seem to be encouraging cooperation between the German colonialists and the missionaries, the Government has asked the Rhenish Missionary Society to train Bushmen, a troublesome element in the community, on their mission farm. Some German farmers, who employ many native labourers, are sending young native Christians to be trained at their expense at the school for native workers at Gaub, with a view to their returning to do evangelistic work on the farms.[29]

It is clear from this quotation that although the training was sometimes done at the expense of the farmers, it was not meant to train the indigenous people to be independent. After completion of their education they were expected to be the assets of the whites.

Coming from German colonialism to South African rule was like jumping from the frying pan into the fire for the Namibians. Although the post-World War I period brought Namibia into the international arena within the League of Nations as Mandate Territory "C", it was not helped in any way thus far. Instead it opened up a new era and form of domination. Colonialism was combined with the apartheid system. It was no longer a question of foreign power only, but now there was also the issue of apartheid, which was maintained by Draconian laws and defended with Scripture passages. Apartheid was thus harder to deal with from the biblical point of view, since the Bible was used to justify it.

Although colonialism and apartheid continued to be felt among the Namibians after World War I, very little is noticeable in the church between the two World Wars. The momentum of the church was increased only after the Second World War. What the church did from then on will be considered in Chapter Four. What can be said in summary is that Namibia was probably the last to be colonized in Africa and will be among the last to be decolonized.

In 1800, very few parts of Africa were under European or other foreign control: a number of tiny coastal enclaves in West, West-Central and East Africa;
a small colony of white settlement in South Africa. Ottoman suzerainty over
North Africa was entirely nominal. Between 1800 and 1940 . . . the whole
of the continent . . . came, for a longer or shorter time, under alien rule. By
the late 1970s nearly all the continent was once again ruled by governments
representing, in some way or another, the indigenous peoples of Africa. The
only remaining exceptions to this are in the extreme south, but even there . . .
changes appear to be on the way. It would seem that it is only a matter of time
before a black government rules Namibia. . . . The future of the Republic of
South Africa remains more imponderable.[30]

Church and Apartheid

"Apartheid" is an Afrikaans word which literally translated
means "apart-ness," "set apart" or "separation." By the early 1940s
Afrikaans newspapers in South Africa already used the term.
Among those government officials who used it was Dr. D.F. Malan, the former (NGK Dutch Reformed Church) minister, news
editor of *Die Burger* and, beginning in 1948, the first National Party
Prime Minister. He "used the term frequently to describe South Africa's goals and system of government."[31]

The central theme of the "apartheid" system is to enforce the separation of races. That is to say, it is a system dedicated to keeping
blacks unintegrated, if possible forever, depriving all people other
than whites of the right to political and economic participation, and
forcing blacks to live in the most arid and peripheral areas of South
Africa and Namibia. This system does not take into consideration
the size of the population of "non-whites." They are seen as "inferior" by the minority "non-colors" or whites who are monop-
olizing the socio-political and economic privileges.

The apartheid system is

a life of privilege, power, and plenty for the whites, based on the exploitation
of cheap "non-white" labor . . . empowered and maintained by iron-fisted
control of four key sectors of South African society, the classical means of any
totalitarian state. They are: 1) the land, 2) the laws, 3) the economy, 4) force.[32]

While the term arouses opprobrium around the globe, at home
it has legitimate authority. Prime Minister J. G. Strijdom, who succeeded Malan in 1954, elaborated on the policy of apartheid in these
terms:

Our policy is that the Europeans must stand their ground and must remain "baas" [boss] in South Africa. If we reject the "herrenvolk" idea and the idea that the white man cannot remain baas, if the franchise is to be extended to the non-Europeans, and if the non-Europeans are developed on the same basis as the Europeans, how can the European remain "baas"? Our view is that in every sphere the Europeans must retain the right to rule the country and keep it a white man's country.[33]

Prime Minister H. F. Verwoerd endorsed it by saying, "We want to keep South Africa white—keeping it white can only mean one thing, namely white domination, not leadership, not guidance, but control, supremacy."[34] This concept was not foreign to Prime Minister B. J. Vorster either (to whom the Namibian Church wrote an Open Letter in 1971), who emphatically said, "South Africa nationhood is for the whites only. That is how I see it, that is how you see it and that is how we will see it for the future."[35]

The entrenchment of the apartheid system has been developed to its highest form since 1948, when it was legalized, but the systematic oppression of the blacks by the whites in every field of life goes all the way back to the white settlement of 1652 and today is being implemented by "apartheid" or "racial separate development"[36] policies.

Namibia has been administered by South Africa since 1915. It was inevitable that apartheid would be extended there also. The Odendaal Commission of 1964 paved the way for the implementation of the policy to its full force in the territory.

South Africa formally imposed its apartheid policy of dividing the country into separate "homelands" on Namibia in 1964. . . . The Odendaal Plan . . . suggested dividing Namibians into twelve "population groups"—whites, Coloureds, Rehoboth Basters, Namas, Damaras, Hereros, Kaokovelders, Ovambos, Kavangos, Caprivians, Tswanas and Bushmen. Each black group, with the exception of the Coloureds, should occupy a "homeland." The "homelands" are Namibian analogues of the South African bantustans.[37]

It should be natural for the Christian Church to react to the way races are socially, economically, geographically, and politically separated, rigidly and compulsorily from one another. But, except for individuals, the church has been silent for too long. It was not until the 1970s that the church was able to issue official statements condemning the policy. Many factors contributed to the evasion of the issue by the church. For example, the church leadership was vested in whites or foreigners who enjoyed the privileges of the white race. German missionaries, as collaborators with the government, could not express any discontent. When South Africa took over the administration, the missionaries (being Germans) were careful not to lose their mission field. The Finnish missionaries were of a pietistic background. For them religion and politics were not to be mixed. They supported a *status quo*. The Anglican Church was not yet established among the indigenous people. Once the Anglican Church was established among the Africans, its position changed by the mid-1940s to that of participation. Michael Scott was one of those who took an active role.

When the leadership of the church was changed and handed over to the Namibians themselves in the 1960s and 1970s, participation of the church became imperative. The joining together of the churches in the formation of the Council of Churches in Namibia was an indication of the willingness of the church to be one voice and concern.

The church was not completely silent, however. *The Missionary Reviews* of 1909 and 1913 reacted to legally prohibited marriages between blacks and German white soldiers. Because of the prohibition, "illegitimate bastard children" were born between these people. This caused a problem to both the missionaries and the government, what the Secretary of the Government Colonies, Mr. Dernburg, has called "the monuments of German shame" in German South West Africa.[38] It was a "shame" because the Germans felt that their white "superior" blood was contaminated by the blacks. These children were left in a twilight zone. Although they were legally seen as blacks, they were at the same time not seen as altogether "inferior," like blacks, but neither "superior," like the whites.

To solve the problem, the German Government adopted a resolution on May 8, 1912 in favor of the legal recognition of marriages between blacks and whites. But it seems there was no intention of enacting the principle into law. The German Colonial Society immediately protested against its adoption.

The executive committee of the society declared itself strictly opposed to all marriages between white and colored persons, demanding at the same time that the government take energetic measures against immoral alliances between members of the two races.[39]

The stand of the Colonial Society was approved by the missionary circles in Germany. It was proposed to establish "bastard" children's asylum schools where they could be educated and sent to church on a regular basis. The boys were to be educated as future German soldiers. The schools were founded by the Rhenish Missionary Society at Okahandja and at Keetmanshoop. *The Missionary Review* proposed without elaboration that "German discipline and the preaching of the Gospel should labor together in eradicating the shame of German South West Africa."[40] Whatever was meant here, another *Missionary Review* indicates that, "while deprecating mixed marriages, both Protestant and Roman Catholic missionary leaders protest strongly against their prohibition."[41]

In 1957 the Synod of the Rhenish Mission Church (RMC), which had been working among various peoples of Namibia, including the whites, constituted the RMC to be the "Evangelical Lutheran Church in South West Africa" (ELC/SWA), a church which was to be inclusive. Unfortunately, the establishment of the ELC/SWA was met with a feeling of "superiority" by some members of the Rehoboth Basters community, because racism has been ingrained into the people of Namibia for too long. This group of people refused to join the new Lutheran Church and instead formed the "Rhenish Congregation," where they felt that their special rights as Basters might not be lost. On the other hand, the white German Lutherans did not join this new church either. They constituted themselves in 1960 as the *Deutsch Evangelische Lutherische Kirche* (DELK—German Evangelical Lutheran Church).

The issue of church and apartheid did not remain an internal issue only; it also affected the church at large externally at the international level. At the Lutheran World Federation's Fourth Assembly in Helsinki in 1963 there was a heated debate on this very issue. Bishop Meyer of Lübeck, Germany questioned why the church in South Africa and Namibia was formed on racial lines. He also foresaw a danger to the church in this region, namely, that it would end up having "two tongues" with regard to the racial discrimination issue. The reaction was given by Bishop Helge Fosseus from South Africa, who seems to have defended the racial system.[42]

Apartheid must be seen as something maintained and sustained by a combined force of clergy and laity, using both the church and the Bible and the power of the state through

mass media for communication to propagate an ideology and promote a social order based on it, which other Christians believe to be incompatible with the Gospel of Jesus Christ. The expulsion of Bishop Mize . . . must be seen then as one Church taking action against another which refuses to accept the ideology of apartheid.[43]

The Open Letter of 1971 was the most important breaking of the church's silence, and the church will probably continue issuing official statements against the policy based on racial segregation. Both in internal and international communities, apartheid has become a moral issue which must be dealt with by both the churches and states. It has been discussed extensively in all major global organizations, including the World Council of Churches (WCC) and the United Nations Organization (UNO).

Recently, the Secretary General of the Council of Churches in Namibia (CCN), Dr. Abisai Shejavali, said:

. . . All people were born equal in God's eyes and that none was made poor or to be oppressed and exploited by others . . . that the creation of separate black locations and homelands was evil and that to demand people to call others "baas" [boss] was a sin. The suffering and inhuman conditions in Namibia were caused by apartheid which made people poor, uneducated and unskilled in their own fatherland. Today Namibians were witnessing the imposition of new masters by a regime south of their border without their consent.[44]

The correct teaching of the church and the principles of apartheid are diametrically opposed. Therefore, apartheid is an immoral, evil, and unacceptable system.

Church and the Migratory Labor System

One has to understand the background and nature of the laws regulating the black population in Namibia since the advent of white rule in the country. The fate of black laborers was decided either by force or by punitive laws. Although blacks had suffered forced labor since 1884, the white people's rule of law with regard to the contract labor system took shape in 1917.

Proclamation No. 3 of 1917 regulates the employment and treatment of Natives on mines and other large works. Employers are required to make written contracts with Natives, which must be attested before a magistrate or other officer. Compound managers must be appointed by the employers to supervise and control the Natives in a compound. . . . Provision is made for the punishment of . . . offences by Natives such as neglect of duty, intoxication, insubordination, breach of health rules, and desertion. . . .[45]

There are also other proclamations, such as Proclamation No. 25 of 1920, which deals with vagrancy of blacks and provides guidance for their punishment, imprisonment, or fine when any one of them is found "wandering abroad." This proclamation was harshly used and made white farmers recipients of "punished" laborers because

the magistrate was required to adjudge a first offender under this law to a term of service on public works or with a private person other than the complainant. . . . The result of this provision was that farmers, needing labour, often waited outside the court to engage offenders of this category.[46]

The Masters and Servants Proclamation No. 34 of 1920 regulating blacks and their white employers' relationships provides further punishment of black laborers even in small matters such as refusing to obey a command of a "master" which the black person feels is contrary to his/her ethics. Those of 1922 were Proclamation No. 11 or Pass Law, which denied blacks the right to "enter or leave the territory nor travel within the territory without a permit," and Proclamation No. 33, prohibiting blacks from being in the streets or public places of any town between 9:00 p.m. and 4:00 a.m. without a pass or permit. Failing to produce the pass meant harassment and detention.

These laws were further worsened by many others, for example, the "Development of Self-Government for Native Nations in South West Africa Act of 1968," which creates the ethnic "homelands." All blacks were forced to give way to allow the whites to occupy ninety percent of the arable and industrial land, although the whites comprise less than ten percent of the total population. Proclamations R.17 of 1972 and AG 9 of 1977 provide further suppression of blacks' feelings and movements by military force.

When speaking of migratory laborers, this law specifically points to black males leaving their families behind in the reserves or "homelands" in order to go to work in the mines, factories and so forth in the so-called white people's area. They are to stay there for twelve to eighteen months in single compounds under the restrictions of the above-mentioned laws and regulations. The "homelands" are established in the areas which are most arid and unproductive. As a result, black males are forced "by economic necessity and oppressive legislation" rather than by desire to "earn extra money for luxuries" to leave the reserves.[47]

Despite the fact that these men leave their families back in the "homelands," they are usually not allowed to choose jobs to their liking or to do what they feel they could do best. Also, the salary is so small that one cannot survive on it. It was said that:

The Ovambo goes to the labour bureau and says, "I am a driver and want work as a driver." He is told, "You are going to build rooms, and the pay is R 5 per week." If he says, "I don't want building work, and I am not satisfied with R 5 per week," he is chased back to Ovambo and there are no means of self-protection.[48]

Very few workers have insurance, pension, or other benefits. The Worker's Compensation Act, which has been in effect in Namibia since 1956, applies only to those workers regarded to be in extremely dangerous working conditions.

Compensation for severe injury and lump sum payments to relatives in case of death are calculated on the basis of previous earnings, which means that black families automatically receive less. . . . A Black would get R400.00 for the loss of an eye, while a White would get R6,000.00 plus other sickness and accident benefits.[49]

Discrimination against people by race or by color is clearly not in keeping with the precepts of Christianity.

We have examined a few of the conditions of black workers outside their "homelands." They are in isolation from their wives, children, friends and neighbors, with no access to visiting them because it would jeopardize their job opportunities. Despite the meager salaries and exposure to dangerous working conditions without any hope for compensation in case of injuries, most black workers cling faithfully to their contract jobs. At the end of their contracts, some go back home with a few pennies in their pockets and others go empty-handed even if their families are patiently and anxiously expecting them to bring something after their twelve–or eighteen–month stays away from home.

When the men go to work, what they leave behind back in the "homelands" are women and children. Voipio says:

It is surprising that Christian marriage has kept its place among the people at all. But one has to remember that the original moral standards of the people were strict and . . .adultery and other forms of immorality [were considered] as serious transgressions.[50]

However, this separation of families has caused serious marital problems.

While men tended to stay with their wives for at least twelve months after marriage during the 1950s, the time between the wedding and the husband's return to work has become shorter. Six months appears to be an average period by the early 1970s, although there are cases of a man only spending several

134

AFRICAN HOMELANDS

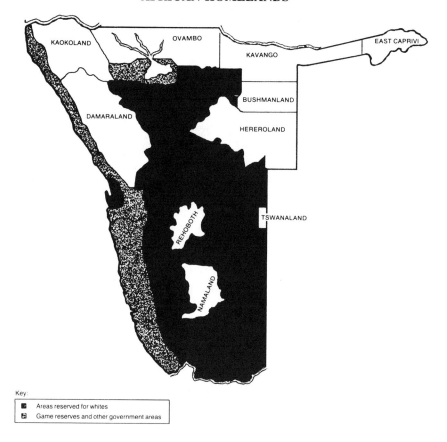

Key:
- Areas reserved for whites
- Game reserves and other government areas

weeks with his wife before returning to contract employment. Often the reason is the hope of being employed again by the same employer. . . . The shortest time between the wedding and the return to work was three weeks. Nevertheless two of the wives state very clearly that their husbands only spent one week at home after the wedding.[51]

The author personally witnessed one of his brothers spending only one week with his wife after the wedding before he returned to his work in order not to lose his job with the same employer. The ultimate result of this marriage was divorce.

Besides separation itself, several factors also play a role in the marital problems caused in this relation. Some of these factors are: the lack of decent housing, money, food, and proper communications. When the husbands go to work, their wives remain behind struggling to survive. They have to keep up with the house and children and get grazing land and water for the animals—goats, sheep, and cattle. They also have to work and cultivate the fields for food and produce enough, usually by hand, for the family. While the wife is expecting the husband to bring along money for blankets and clothing and additional necessities, the husband on his part is expecting to find food at home through the labor of his wife. When these expectations are not met, the result often is a marriage crisis, because neither one of the two could easily understand why his or her partner did not make it.

Other family problems are caused by the lack of communication. There are no telephones through which husbands and wives or young men and their parents can talk to one another during the twelve months of absence. The national illiteracy rate of about seventy percent does not facilitate the regular exchange of letters. To find a friend who can help in writing is not always easy either. Even in cases where that is possible, one does not express herself or himself as one would if writing on her/his own. News from home and from work is often late. Even cases of death are often heard of too late, sometimes after several days, weeks, or even months.

The separation of families causes wives to experience lonely lives, exhaustion from overworking, and the most unbearable conditions of marital life. The effects of this separation on men are the same. Meager wages and lack of financial benefits prevent them from supporting their families. It is financially impossible, even if they were to work days and nights without rest. Traveling harassments, labor bureaucracies, long days of work, unthinkable and inhuman conditions in the single compounds, which are often raided by police, and the prohibition against forming workers' unions have caused black migrant workers to live a life of slavery. Homosexuality, caused by long absences from wives, has been reported in the single compounds. Although this practice does not occur on a large scale, it is, nevertheless, a new form of deviation from the Namibian traditional way of life. Above all:

The effect of the migrant labour system on family life is one of the most traumatic consequences of the apartheid economy. . . . The majority of the black labour force live involuntarily and unnaturally as single men for the greater part of their lives while their wives and children remain in the reserves, supporting themselves on subsistence agriculture.[52]

Too many years have passed with the migratory labor system in effect, and there seems to be less hope than ever of changing the system under the current government. The workers have periodically rebelled, beginning with a major general strike on December 2, 1893 at Gross Otavi mine. There was further restlessness between 1915 and 1972. A revolutionary national movement, the South West Africa People's Organization (SWAPO) was organized in 1960. The workers have called upon the church to help them in their problems. The church must react to this call.

The church abhors the migratory labor system, but very little was said by the church for many years. Probably the lead was taken by the Anglican Church, which through its uncompromising attitude toward the evil societal practices perpetrated and perpetuated by the apartheid government in Namibia lost three successive bishops and a pastor, viz., Bishop Robert Mize (1968), Bishop Colin O'Brien Winter (1972), Bishop Richard Wood (1975) and the Rev. Edward Morrow (1978), plus many other workers as well. In support of the workers' strike of 1971–72 and his outspoken stand against the overall apartheid system, discrimination against blacks, and the practice of racism on the part of the government, Bishop Winter was expelled from Namibia in 1972.

The voice of the Lutheran Church expressed itself in the Open Letter of June 30, 1971 to Mr. B. J. Vorster, the then Prime Minister of South Africa, and categorically stated in Article Five that:

Through the application of Job Reservation the right to a free choice of profession is hindered and this causes low remuneration and unemployment. There can be no doubt that the contract system breaks up a healthy life because the prohibition of a person from living where he works, hinders the cohabitation of families. This conflicts with Section 23 and 25 of the Human Rights.[53]

The letter was supported by other churches in the country, both in theory and in practice. Since then, the silence of the church, on this matter as well as on other social and political issues, was broken. The church felt the need to express its opinions in matters that required social and political change as part of its message of hope in a dehumanized society. For the uncompromising participation of the church in the struggle of the people for change, it suffered the consequences of harassments, detentions, expulsion and even killing of its workers, destruction of its property, and resentment from the illegal occupying government. However, in the struggle to restore healthy family lives, humanly acceptable working conditions, peace, and justice in the territory, the church has become a witness to martyrdom. In fact, the church has become a threat in the eyes of the evil society. The more adamantly the government is against change, the more difficult it becomes for the church to even speak of reconciliation. Forgiveness and reconciliation are only possible when both parties realize the wrong incurred. The migratory labor system will remain immoral until it becomes a voluntary practice depending on the individual workers' freedom of choice. It is also true that any change in Namibia today without the backing of the workers is doomed to fail. Therefore, the black labor force remains a power to reckon with in the process of change. The church cannot ignore this formidable segment of its body. It must listen to cries for support and assistance where possible.

In 1981 the Rev. Gerson Max, who has been working among the migrant workers for many years and once was President of the Namibia National Union, said:

There was still considerable discrimination in industry, making it difficult for black workers to obtain the wages or conditions that their work merited. Whilst the management at Rossing [uranium mine] could speak of the rate for the job, irrespective of race, and living conditions to match, the reality was found in the restriction of black workers to Arandis, the black township, whatever their skill or grade. The way forward in the improvement of wages and conditions for black workers is in unionisation but considerable difficulties are encountered in any attempts at effective unionisation. There are worker councils and registered unions but these are committees without teeth and act in the employers' interests. Whenever effective unions are formed bannings and detentions are used to get rid of leaders and undermine the attempts at organisation.[54]

For Max, the pastoral aspects of the gospel and practical and political caring of the people of God flow together. "For this reason the application of the gospel becomes a cause of suffering."[55]

Workers' Strikes in Namibia[56]
1915–1972

Year	Place	Other Known Details
1916		Migrant workers strike for issue of working clothes.
1916	Kahn mine	Manager misleads Government in attempt to get police to intimidate workers.

Workers' Strikes in Namibia[56]
1915–1972

1918	Farms	Workers down tools in protests.
1923	Lüderitz mines	Workers retaliate when one of them assaulted by foreman. Seventeen workers fined.
1925	Conception Bay	Strike threatened: 13 "ringleaders" arrested.
1937	Oranjemund mine	Miners strike in protest over start of X-ray examinations for pilfered diamonds of departing migrant workers.
1939	Tsumeb mine	Strike by workers who suspect not receiving pay they are entitled to.
1939	Nageib mine	
Sep. 1948	Tsumeb mine	2,000 strike in protest when 13-year-old white shoots dead one African worker.
1952	Lüdertiz	Cannery workers(?) Large strike.
1953	Lüdertiz	Fish cannery strikes; three workers shot dead by police.
1953	Walvis Bay	Fish cannery strikes.
1953	Tsumeb	Copper smelter workers strike over furnace working conditions.
1954	A copper mine	
1956	Brandberg mine	
1956	Otjisondu mine	
c. 1956	Windhoek	Laundry washerwomen strike.

Workers' Strikes in Namibia[56]
1915–1972

1959	Walvis Bay	Oceana Fish Cannery. Go-slow strike over (a) foreman's assaults and attempts to force workers to clean dangerous machinery while in motion; (b) wages; (c) 12 or 18 hour working day; (d) other working conditions.
June 1962	Walvis Bay	Large strike; 55 arrested; fined L30 or three months jail (L30 was then between 3–9 months wages).
1968	Walvis Bay	Fish cannery workers strike, over 1,000 for over three weeks. Want night shift paid at overtime rate.
Apr. 1971	Walvis Bay & Lüderitz(?)	Cannery strikes.
13 Dec. 1971– Jan. 1972	General strike	Over 13,500 mostly migrant workers strike against whole system of pass laws, migrant labor under criminal indenture.
Feb. 1972	Walvis Bay	Cannery workers against "pig food," concrete beds, and migrant labor system.
Feb. 1972	Otjiwarongo	Municipal workers strike for wage rise.

NOTES

1. Matthew 28:19-20.
2. Stephen Neill, *Colonialism and Christian Missions* (New York: McGraw-Hill Book Co., 1966), 11.

3. William Loren Katz, *Eyewitness: The Negro in American History* (New York: Pitman Publishing Corp., 1967), 5.

4. Ibid.

5. Neill, 390.

6. Roland Oliver and Anthony Atmore, *Africa Since 1800* (London, 1981), 107.

7. Ibid., 103.

8. Ibid., 200.

9. Ibid., 110–11.

10. H. Loth, cited in Horst Drechsler, *Let Us Die Fighting* (Zed Press, 1980), 18.

11. Lukas J. de Vries, *Mission and Colonialism in Namibia* (Johannesburg, 1978), 73.

12. Drechsler, 19.

13. Ibid.

14. Neill, 388–89.

15. Ibid., 392.

16. Ibid., 393.

17. C. P. Groves. *The Planting of Christianity in Africa,* vol. 3 (London, 1955), 64.

18. Randolph Vigne, *A Dwelling Place of our Own,* 10. See also Ruth First, *South West Africa,* 73–74; and Robin Hallet, *Africa Since 1875,* 622.

19. *The Missionary Review of the World* (1905), 317.

20. Drechsler, 214.

21. Robin Hallet, *Africa Since 1875* (University of Michigan, 1974), 623.

22. *International Review of Missions* (1916), 55.

23. Groves, 3:67–68.

24. G. Warneck, cited in Elsie Singmaster, *The Story of Lutheran Missions* (Columbia, SC: Press of Survey Publishing Co., 1917), 130–31.

25. Groves, 4:22.

26. *The Year 1915—International Review of Missions* (1916), 55.

27. First, 90.

28. Colin Winter, *Namibia* (Wm. B. Eerdman's Publishing Co., 1977), 15.

29. *The Year 1914—International Review of Missions* (1915), 48.

30. Oliver and Atmore, 315.

31. Louis Stack and Don Morton, *Torment to Triumph in Southern Africa* (New York: Friendship Press, 1976), 17.

32. Ibid., 18–19.

33. Ibid., 18.

34. Ibid., 18–19.

35. Ibid., 19.

36. Cf. Basil Davidson, *A History of East and Central Africa* (New York: Anchor Books, 1969), 281–87.

37. *Namibia: The Facts* (London: IDAF for Southern Africa, 1980), 15.

38. *The Missionary Review of the World* (1909), 955.

39. *The Missionary Review of the World* (1913), 556.

40. Ibid.

41. *International Review of Missions* (1912), 47.

42. See *Report of the Lutheran World Federation (LWF), 4th Assembly* (Helsinki: July 30–August 11, 1963), 62–63.

43. *The International Review of Missioins* (1969), 47.

44. See *The Namibian* (Windhoek, July 18, 1986).

45. John H. Wellington, *South West Africa and its Human Issues* (Oxford: Clarendon Press, 1967), 282.

46. Ibid.

47. Gillian and Suzanne Cronje, *The Workers of Namibia* (London: IDAF, 1979), 21.

48. Ibid., 33. (*Note:* R5 is equivalent to $5 USA)

49. Ibid., 48.

50. Rauha Voipio, "Contract Work through Ovambo Eyes," in *Namibia: The Last Colony,* ed. Reginald H. Green, Kimmo Kiljunen, and Marja-Liisa Kiljunen (Longman, 1981), 114.

51. Ibid., 115.

52. Cronje, 36–37.

53. See "Open Letter" to Prime Minister Mr. B. J. Vorster of June 30, 1971.

54. "Namibia: A Nation Wronged," the report of a visit to Namibia by a delegation sent by the British Council of Churches at the invitation of the Council of Churches in Namibia, 16 to 28 November 1981, 18–19.

55. Ibid., 19.

56. Source: Cronje, 78–79.

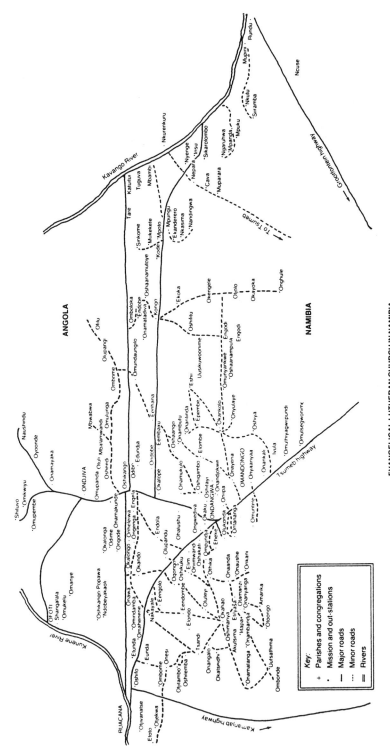

EVANGELICAL LUTHERAN CHURCH IN NAMIBIA
Source: ELCIN ARCHIVES

Key:
+ Parishes and congregations
· Mission and out-stations
— Major roads
··· Minor roads
= Rivers

ANGOLA

NAMIBIA

Kunene River

RUACANA

Kamanjab highway

Tsumeb highway

Kavango River

Grootfontein highway

To Tsumeb

Ncuse

Rundu

From Colonialism to Nationalism in Namibia

IV

R eligion and politics are not separable in Namibian tradition. Very often a king or chief has been both a religious and a political leader. In some communities, men and women held this position equally. Moreover, the terms "religion" and "politics" do not exist in Namibian languages, because every person was both a religious and a political being. Therefore, there was no need for the terms to exist; and even if they did exist, they would have little value. However, through foreign influence there are now terms being used to refer to religion or politics. But the concept continues to be confusing when people try to set them apart.

When Christianity was introduced to the Namibians 181 years ago, it was under a strong pietistic attitude of rigid separation of religion and politics—something contrary to the Namibian understanding. European theology was expert in dichotomizing life. Life was divided into things sacred (religious) and things secular (political), but, nevertheless, the preaching referred to God as being everywhere, and it was heresy to teach that there are times when God is absent. The contradiction was almost never seen. Jesus put it correctly when he said, "I am with you always," meaning that God is ever present. It is important, though, to point out that God's presence does not mean that God endorses anything. Therefore, it is possible and necessary to challenge evil practices.

Religion is defined as "belief in a divine being or beings." Some defined it as an ideological system based on a belief in spiritual beings or forces not subject to empirical investigation.[1] Whatever the definition, Namibians had been religious even before Christianity was brought to them.

Politics is defined as "theory and conduct of government" or theories and methods to conduct government affairs. According to Claude Phillips, all societies, no matter how primitive, have their own kind of political systems governed by three main settings: 1) a technological setting with its various natures depending on the context; 2) a sociological setting, which includes various shapes of social organizations and structures, such as families or clans; 3) an ideological or psychological setting based on systems of belief, values and attitudes.[2] Let us consider Namibia in the context of these settings and their wider definitions.

Every individual exists within the limits of those settings. But politics is further defined as "the process by which authoritative decisions are made for a society; the process for authoritatively resolving conflict or making decisions for a society."[3] The system used for certain people to acquire positions of decision-making depends on each context. In pre-colonial Namibia this was done in many ways. It was achieved by inheritance, appointment, election, or tradition. Today it is done through the imposition of puppet leaders. However, the collective method most aspired to is free and fair election.

If the definitions of religion and politics are accurate, and both religious and political leaders are elected through similar electoral procedures, then it becomes very hard for Namibians to understand the "parrot cry" that religion and politics should not be mixed. The contact with Europeans split the role of the king or chief between two people—one represented religion and the other represented politics. Contrary to the cry of not mixing religion and politics, the very same people are violating it at the same time by voting for their own political leaders and social managers. Even if all people became Christians, it would always be imperative that people would continue to need political structures, simply because they are not in heaven yet.

In this way the theological thinking and mentality of the Namibians has been colonized along with the rest of the society. With the rise of nationalism and a strong current of desire for self-determination, there is a noticeable shift in the thinking of Namibian theologians. It has become necessary for them to reject whatever is too foreign for them in both theological understanding and political analysis. They are tired of keeping religion and politics separated in such a way that the two have nothing in common. They used to receive as true whatever the Europeans said, but now they are attempting to put their thinking into the contexts of Namibian culture, history, and tradition.

As to why Namibians now refuse to separate religion and politics, Bishop Bonifatius Haushiku explains:

There are many people accusing the church of meddling in politics. They want the so-called pure church which has nothing to do with material preoccupations. To-day I want to answer these people by saying that the Church of God is for [people] and [people] are the Church; and [a person] is not a purely spiritual being, he or she has a body which is material and must also be the concern of the Church. A Church which does not look at this dimension of [a person] is a church working in the clouds and its religion is that which some people would like to call "the opium of the people." Such a religion is foreign to the Africa continent.[4]

Bishop Haushiku believes that the church ought to involve itself in ministry to the whole person's needs — spiritually, morally, politically, socially, economically, and educationally. He is one of many theologians in the country who have a similar understanding.

The political conscience of the Namibian people is aroused. Whenever they meet they talk about nationalist politics, colonial liberation, and the role of God in societal concerns. This is indicative that in Namibia religion and politics have become a preoccupation. In doing this, they are in fact occupying themselves with what life is all about.

INDIGENIZATION OF THE CHURCH

What is meant by indigenization of the church can be understood from the definition of the term "indigenous." According to Webster's dictionary, "indigenous" is defined as "produced, growing, or living naturally in a country or climate; native." A church, therefore, which is not intimately connected to the local people both in its theology and ethics and in its leadership and organization cannot be seen as an indigenous church. In order to become indigenized, the church has to bear the natural flavor of the context. In other words, the church needs to be contextualized if it is to fulfill the needs of the people. Any imposed system cannot properly serve the aim it intended to achieve.

The traditional explanation of the indigenous church is when that church is *self-governing, self-supporting,* and *self-propagating.* A fourth which could also be added is *self-criticizing.*

In terms of self-governance, with regard to the purpose and importance of church organization, the missionaries tried to make carbon copies their churches of origin. They wanted African churches to be like the ones in their countries both in shape and in structure. As it turned out, their aims produced the serious problem of a great delay in allowing indigenous people to take part in leadership. The missionaries monopolized everything for much too long. As a result, secessions took place at different stages. Some of the reasons for this were that in many ways church organization has been either complicated or boring for the Africans. The Africans ended up tamed or conforming to whatever came, even if they did not find it interesting and appealing to them. When the leadership was opened up for the indigenous people, church structures were too complicated to run without the money which used to come from abroad. These funds were drastically cut as soon as the missionaries gave way to indigenous leaders.

Self-support has to do with salaries, property and its maintenance, as well as expenses in doing various activities within the church. The independence of most Namibians disappeared with the coming of the missionaries. Namibians were either confined to mission colonies or introduced to new ways of life which were no longer productive. Liquor was ruthlessly poured into the country by traders who came at the same time as the missionaries. The system by which the church was organized was based on the context in which people were working and earning cash to maintain themselves and their families. Economic exploitation was enhanced with the advent of colonial rule. People lost their former properties and were denied new ones; they were also denied access to the land. At the same time, more and more people became Christians and were required to give at least a tenth from that with which they were not even able to buy bread for themselves. Namibians became victims of the structures both within and outside the church.

As a result of all this, when the churches were declared "independent," it was just a word. Financially they remained dependent on their mother churches or mission societies. This will continue to be so until one of the following is done: the structure of the church is altered, or Namibia is free politically and economically. A church cannot be independent if the country is taken hostage by social evils. Under the current structure of the churches in Namibia there is room for the church to exploit its workers both physically and economically. Therefore, the church would like to see a free society because that would help the extension of church activities.

Self-propagation is tied to the two afore-mentioned points. When there is no free, normal functioning of society, there is no free normal functioning of the church, even if the church represents the majority of the populace. Giving moral support without concrete actions is not always a good way to accomplish tasks. The vision of the church cannot be transformed into action without material supplements.

Self-criticism is also important. A church which does not criticize and revise itself may run the danger of losing its goal. Critical analysis of the church can save the church from unnecessary preoccupations.

By indigenization I mean contextualization, and by contextualization of the church I mean making the church understood by the people it serves at a particular point in time without losing the kernel of its identity, content, and global nature.

If the church in Namibia is to succeed, it needs to be independent of foreign aid in managing its affairs. At this time it can be independent in leadership, but due to the reasons mentioned above, it cannot be financially independent. It is also necessary to apply and simplify the gospel message within the Namibian context. Communication of the gospel needs to be done through Namibian understanding, traditional music, proverbs, poetry, figures and expressions of speech which carry the values of the people.[5] The church in Namibia cannot continue things simply because others are doing them if they do not carry any meaning to the people. Uniformity is crucial to the faith, but imitation for the sake of being accepted leads to hypocrisy and neo-colonialism even within the church.

THE QUEST FOR UNITY

Despite resentments which prevailed among the different missionary societies, it cannot be denied that cooperation existed among them in the planting of Christianity in Namibia. Here, however, we are more interested in the more organized cooperation in the history of the church in Namibia, and will now attempt to highlight the story of that organized cooperation.

J. T. Potgieter was a Dutch Reformed Church minister at Mariental, in the Gibeon Circuit. He had an ecumenical vision of mission and was one of the first notable people to take an initiative towards cooperation among churches. In 1941 Potgieter invited Rev. Birger Eriksson of the Finnish Mission in Ovamboland to attend the first Gibeon Circuit meeting. The Rhemish Mission was also approached in this connection. The burning issue here was the Ovambo contract laborers in the south, especially on white farms

The three churches—namely, the DRC, FMS, and RMS—had to do something if these men were ever to be helped. They were mostly from the north, where the FMS was working. In 1941 the matter was discussed without any concrete steps towards action being taken. Four years later a preliminary agreement was achieved at Engela when Potgieter, S.H. van der Spuy, and Schutte went to Ovambo for that purpose. The final agreement among the three churches—the Finnish Mission (later ELCIN-ELOC), the Rhenish Mission (later ELCSWA) and the DRC—was reached at Karibib on May 9, 1947. It was called the "Driehoek" (Triangle) Agreement because of its three representatives. It was to undertake responsibility for spiritual care to tens of thousands of contract workers from Ovamboland working in the south. The different churches or missions were represented as follows: J. T. Potgieter, C. A. Gagiano, and elder R. F. Odendaa represented the DRC; F. Alho and Birger Eriksson represented the FMS; and H. Vedder and F. Pönnighaus came from the Rhenish Mission.[6]

The responsibility of each was that the Finnish Mission would provide literature and train evangelists for that work; the Rhenish Mission would provide buildings free of charge for conducting services; while the DRC would take care of salaries, transportation, and accommodations.

This cooperation continued even beyond the time when the ELCIN and ELCSWA were constituted as independent churches—in 1954 and 1957 respectively. With the view of starting its own independent mission work among the blacks, the DRC Synod of 1969 decided to break the Driehoek Agreement. The two remaining churches could not continue on the same basis, so the Driehoek became another detail in the history of Christianity in Namibia.

When the Dutch Reformed Church broke its Driehoek Agreement with the two Lutheran churches in 1969, these two churches—the Evangelical Lutheran Church in South West Africa (ELCSWA) and the Evangelical Lutheran Ovambo-Kavango Church (ELOC, later ELCIN)—decided to establish their own new agreement to further the work previously done by Driehoek.

Since three Lutheran churches do exist in the country—two for blacks and one for whites—efforts toward cooperation had been undertaken even before the Driehoek Agreement was broken. In 1961 such an effort toward cooperation was considered at the

"Conference of the Three Lutheran Churches in South West Africa."[8] Thereafter the Church Councils of the three churches met each year to discuss and explore issues of common concern.

One of the results of these gatherings was the amalgamation of the two black Lutheran seminaries into one, United Lutheran Theological Seminary, Paulinum in 1963. Five years later the joint meeting of the ELCSWA and ELCIN Church Councils decided to move a step ahead towards complete union. Both the ELCSWA Synod of July 2, 1970 at Otjimbingwe and the extra Synod of the ELCIN of January 15, 1971 at Ongwediva approved the move.

Meanwhile, the other Lutheran church, the GELCSWA (DELK), also decided to join the negotiations towards union in 1969, but within less than a year it withdrew. On March 2, 1972 the move was taken at Otjimbingwe by the two black Lutheran churches to form the "United Evangelical Lutheran Church in South West Africa" (UELCSWA). Bishop L. Auala of the ELCIN became its first president (1973–75), followed by J. Lukas de Vries (1975–78), Bishop K. Dumeni (1978–83), Bishop Hendrik Fredrik (1983–86) and now Wilfried Blank (1986–   ).

According to the UELCSWA Constitution, the union was on a federal basis rather than a complete union. However, they were to strive for full unity and merger of the Lutheran churches in the country into one Lutheran church.

After the formation of the federation, the German Lutherans continued to be hesitant about joining the UELCSWA. One of the main reasons was that the UELCSWA participated in the socio-political witness in the country's crisis. In 1975 the GELCSWA applied for membership. The other two UELCSWA members were, at this time, hesitant to accept the application. Although the application was accepted at one time, it was soon withdrawn and was withheld until 1977 when the GELCSWA removed its major condition for joining the inter–racial body. This condition was the twin demand of "non-interference in political issues" and of keeping the UELCSWA only on a federal basis rather than striving for future merger.

Even after the GELCSWA was accepted into UELCSWA membership, it continued to be supportive of the *status quo*. As a result, the GELCSWA was one of the churches suspended from LWF at Budapest, Hungary in 1984. During the suspension period, the

GELCSWA seemed to speak up against the socio–political evils of apartheid, although keeping a relatively low profile. In 1986 the leader of the GELCSWA, Landespropst Wilfried Blank, was elected president of the UELCSWA. Presently, there are negotiations underway toward merger of the three Lutheran churches in Namibia—1992 at the earliest.

Colonization and nationalism are matters confined not only to politics. These trends have also been observed within the church. A church under colonialism of another church is not free to decide what is necessary for its context. Such a church cannot speak what is contextual without provoking the colonialist church. In the above section, "Indigenization of the Church," we observed that a particular church in a particular country can claim to be independent only if it is self–governing, self–supporting, self–propagating, and able to shape its organization by self-criticism.

For a long time the church in Namibia has been divided by denominationalism. Families have been divided because members belong to different churches which will have nothing to do with each other. The traditions separating Roman Catholics and Protestants persist even in Namibia, often without any reason as to why this should be the case.

We can speak here of mental colonialism in the church. These divisions are not Namibian creations. They were brought to us. Then we clung to them blindly simply because the different missionaries told us to be different. The unifying message of the Bible was ignored by preoccupation with these divisions.

It is necessary to say all this in view of the membership of the Council of Churches in Namibia. The Council serves as an example of the attempt to keep the traditions of each church while at the same time maintaining the importance of the Church as one body. The process towards closer cooperation among churches was speeded up not only by a movement of opposition to political colonialism and oppression, but also by the process of indigenization of the church. In 1960 all churches in the country were under foreign leadership. The ELCIN was the first to elect an indigenous leader, in 1960. Some other "mainline" churches followed in indigenizing their leadership.

Indigenous leaders have sought to cooperate with other churches. The quest for unity is a necessity both to form Christian fellowship among Christians of different churches and to combat oppression and colonialism.

To make this vision practical, a Christian Center was established in Windhoek. One of its services was to dispatch information to churches. Although we do not have much information at hand on how all this was done, the Christian Center is usually referred to as a forerunner of the Council of Churches in Namibia.[9] The Council was organized in 1977, constituted formally in 1978, and officially opened in 1979.

The membership of the Council of Churches in Namibia includes:

1. African Methodist Episcopal Church (AMEC)
2. Anglican Church—Diocese of Namibia
3. United Congregational Church
4. Evangelical Lutheran Church in Namibia (ELCIN-ELOC)
5. Evangelical Lutheran Church in Namibia/South West Africa (ELCSWA-Rhenish Mission)
6. Methodist Church
7. German Evangelical Lutheran Church in South West Africa (GELCSWA)
8. Roman Catholic Church—The Vicariate of Windhoek
9. Evangelical Reformed Church (as an observer).

The Council is headed by Bishop James H. Kauluma of the Anglican Church, who serves as its president. Dr. Abisai Shejavali is its secretary general. The CCN also has various departments, each with its own director. They include:

1. Theology and Youth
2. Communication (publishes *CCN-Information* newsletter)
3. Education
4. Rural Development
5. Social and Diaconic Programme
6. Administration and Finance

One of the goals of the CCN is to contextualize theology and to seek for holistic service to meet the needs of God's people both physically and spiritually. There are still many problems to be overcome so that the Council of Churches in Namibia can withstand challenges and reach its objectives.

Namibian Politics

It is a disservice to the history of Namibia to bypass politics at this point in time. Colonialism has been felt not only in the church, but even more so in the political arena. The political quest for unity can be traced to the nineteenth–century pre–colonial Namibian leaders. At the time of colonization these leaders felt the violation of their rights. In 1888 Chief Hendrik Witbooi wrote a letter to Chief Maharero calling for unity among the chiefs against the onslaught of German colonialism. He wrote: "By colour and way of life we belong together . . . [our] separate kingdoms and territories is an insignificant subdivision."[10] Witbooi realized that those differences were insignificant when unity was at stake.

Colonialism, which brought disunity to Namibia, was seen as evil by both colonized and colonists alike. The second German governor in Namibia, Theodor Leutwein (1894–1904), wrote:

Colonization . . . is always inhuamne. It must ultimately amount to an encroachment on the rights of the original inhabitants in favor of the intruders. If that is unacceptable then one must oppose all colonisation. . . . What is impossible is on the one hand to take land from the natives on the basis of questionable treaties and risk the life and health of one's countrymen to this end, and on the other to enthuse about humanitarian principles in the Reichtag.[11]

It is true that colonization is inhumane and needs to be abolished. The Namibians were correct to challenge it in the late nineteenth and early twentieth centuries. That challenge still continues through some of the political groups and organizations. We shall only mention two of those organizations.

The South West Africa National Union (SWANU) was founded in 1959 with the intent of uniting the people of Namibia into one national front. To summarize its objectives it says:

To unite and rally the people of South West Africa into one national front, to organize the common people, workers and peasants, of South West Africa and lead them in the struggle for national independence and self-determination; to work with allied movement in Africa for the propagation and promotion of the concept of Pan-Africanism and unity amongst the people of Africa.[12]

How to transform words into action is not an easy task. SWANU was faced with the problem of action and national organization. It lacked both strategies and international recognition. In the 1960s SWANU was briefly recognized by the OAU, but this recognition ceased in 1965. While other African liberation movements were taking up arms, SWANU decided to keep aloof from such struggles of confrontation on the battle front. Because of this lack of tactics, SWANU's popularity quickly declined. Although it remained solely an internal organization, there are now two factions: One faction is led by Moses Katjiuongua, who is collaborating with the South African administration in the Multi-Party Conference (MPC). The other faction, led by Kuzeeko Kangueehi, remains opposed to the *status quo* and has called for UN Resolution 435 to be implemented. SWANU is running the risk of being seen as primarily tribally affiliated and thereby of losing the support of those from across the whole of the national spectrum.

South West Africa People's Organization (SWAPO) was founded in 1960. As SWANU was organized among the students and intellectuals, SWAPO was organized among the students and workers. SWAPO is defined in the constitution as:

. . . a national liberation movement rallying together, on the basis of free and voluntary association, all freedom-inspired sons and daughters of the Namibian people. It is the organized political vanguard of the oppressed and exploited people of Namibia. In fulfilling its vanguard role, SWAPO organizes, unites, inspires, orients and leads the broad masses of the working Namibian people in the struggle for national and social liberation. It is thus the expression and embodiment of national unity, of a whole people united and organized in the struggle for total independence and social liberation.[13]

Like SWANU, SWAPO's aim is the unification of all people of Namibia into one national political organization, and, ultimately, to maintain real African independence. SWAPO has had to face the question of how to keep words consistent with action. The issue of strategy and methodology confronted SWAPO as well. There were two directions to take: to adopt the option of a non–armed struggle, the effectiveness of which was at the mercy of the prevailing laws of the country; or to take up arms to bring about decolonization despite the critical suffering involved. SWAPO took the latter course out of necessity. This was done after SWAPO had exhausted all other options. Although this organization took up arms, it was done out of love and the respect for human life. The following description from SWAPO's newsletters gives us a better definition of the stand of the organization:

To safeguard peace and to prevent war, all the forces that are committed to the future of world progress should rally against the military danger. . . .

SWAPO and, before that, individual Namibians, had carried out for decades a long peaceful struggle through demonstrations and petitions asking for the restoration of the rights of Namibians. These were not heeded. And not only that, peaceful protesters were met with brutal repression and killings. *It was only as a last resort that SWAPO created PLAN (People's Liberation Army of Namibia) and launched the armed struggle.*[14]

In waging guerrilla war SWAPO does not mean that the people involved condone killing. They want to preserve life at all costs, but they are forced to kill by the system itself. The following will again highlight this point:

Even in the commitment of the people of Namibia to armed struggle they must never forget that they are human beings who have been forced by an evil system to have to kill other human beings and that they seek a new society where the chain of the oppressor will be broken. For SWAPO then, the commitment to armed struggle is motivated by a deep love for humanity and by the urgency of destroying the apartheid regime and building a new society in Namibia.[15]

SWAPO, in the process of action towards national liberation, won itself recognition on the international platform. In the mid-1960s the Organization of African Unity (OAU) recognized SWAPO as having the criteria and qualities of a liberation movement. One of those criteria is the waging of guerrilla warfare against colonial powers. As SWAPO remains Namibia's only recognized liberation movement, the United Nations General Assembly of 1973 recognized SWAPO as the authentic representative of the Namibian people. SWAPO is also the only liberation movement to be given full observer status at the UN General Assembly and participation rights in all UN agencies.[16] This status was given in 1976.

Under the leadership of its president, Sam Nuuyoma, SWAPO has been waging guerrilla warfare since August 26, 1966. As a commitment to the national unity of SWAPO, Dr. Sam Nuuyoma is quoted as saying that in Namibia,

we have tribal differences, but we shall and we must overcome them. For me my best brother, my best sister is one with whom I share the same political lot and the same political opinion. My real brother is he who is ready, as I am, to shed his blood for our common cause. That is, for the ideal that our country should be free from racialism, colonialism and foreign exploitation.[17]

SWAPO has become the decisive and formidable force in the struggle for national independence. SWAPO not only resorted to armed struggle, but is firmly committed to the education of Namibians in many fields of study. The future of Namibia depends greatly on SWAPO, because only in SWAPO do we have well-qualified people in many areas. However, these people are deterred from coming to Namibia by the colonial power in the country. On the other hand, we should note that SWANU (progressive), SWAPO, the churches and other groups of people in Namibia are collectively calling for the implementation of UNSC Resolution 435 in Namibia. SWAPO is ever ready to sign a cease-fire with South Africa. There will be no solution to the Namibia issue without the participation of SWAPO. SWAPO (D), which is an offshoot of SWAPO and currently a collaborator with South Africa in the MPC's Transitional Government's effort to bypass Resolution 435 of the UN, should join hands with the progressive forces. Otherwise, SWAPO (D) has a limited vision of Namibian nationalism.

The most recent historical event in the quest for national unity was the /Ai-//Gams Conference. This conference was organized by the Council of Churches in Namibia to bring together all the supporters of UN Resolution 435. Those who participated in this historic first conference were churches, political parties, and several groups of people seeking a genuine solution to their country's long-standing problem. The conference was organized and met in Windhoek on April 29–30, 1986. The outcome of the conference was the adoption of a declaration known as the "/Ai-//Gams Declaration." The declaration rejects and protests against delaying tactics being played by South Africa and the United States of America towards the implementation of UNSC Resolution 435. It also rejects the linkage of Cuban troops in Angola to the Namibia issue. The puppet interim government in Namibia, the violation of human rights, and the illegal presence of the South African Army in the country are all rejected by the declaration.

The /Ai-//Gams Declaration reaffirms the call for Namibia's immediate independence, commitment to an undivided Namibia—one Namibia, one nation—and the international status of Namibia, and sees Resolution 435 as the only democratic means left towards independence for Namibia. The Declaration ends with a vow to mobilize the Namibian masses in resistance to the status quo.

The /Ai-//Gams Conference demonstrated the cataclysm of the Namibian sense of national unity irrespective of race, color, or religion. One is tempted to say that the /Ai-//Gams Conference was the beginning of a new era of a combined effort of Namibians to strive for a Namibia which is free and unified. True nationalism is only possible when all citizens work together. However, it is still too early to see the results of the implementation of the /Ai-//Gams Declaration.

The Church in Exile

Namibia has experienced a tradition of the church in exile. Europeans brought the church to us, they were also the ones who exiled the church outside Namibia. This statement cannot be understood until the following historical sketch is understood.

In 1904, when the Herero insurrection broke out, many Herero people were either maimed, gunned down, starved in Omaheke, or forced to flee Namibia into neighboring Botswana. These fugitives wandered through Botswana as far as Lake Ngami, where most settled. A number of them reached the Zambezi River. These refugees and displaced Namibians had been christianized by the "same" Germans years before. Despite their displacement, they did not lose their Christian faith and identity.

In 1919–20 some Lutheran missionaries of the Hermannsburg Mission from northern Transvaal in South Africa came to Botswana. The missionaries visited these refugees and found that these Namibians had built a village. Among the village houses was a little church. An evangelist (presumably from Namibia) named Ephraim and a deacon named Timothy took care of the people's spiritual needs. When the missionaries arrived, they could see the love that these people had for the gospel, despite their lot. As a result, the missionaries decided to stay with them for two weeks. During the two weeks fifty adults and sixty-one children were baptized. On the baptismal day the refugees collected a thank-offering of $175.00, which they gave to the missionaries to take with them.[18]

Since the 1960s many Namibians of all ages have been exiled because of political repressions and ruthless detentions. The case of Father Shimbonde is a typical example. Father Stephen Shimbonde, formerly a parish priest of the Anglican Church of St. Luke at Epinga, together with some members of his parish, moved to

Angola some years ago. This was the only way for him to escape the intimidations of the South African armed forces in northern Namibia. Now Pastor Shimbonde is leading a parish called "Epinga-across-the-border," exiled in the south of Angola. Whenever he tries to visit his people inside Namibia, he always encounters assaults from the South African soldiers.

Due to wide-scale repression and the introduction of compulsory military service by the illegal occupying regime, between 70,000 and 100,000 Namibians fled the country and live in exile. Except for a very small number, all of them are under the care of SWAPO. They are hosted by many countries, once again including Botswana. Botswana has given assistance to the Namibian refugees since the early 1900s.

These refugees are mostly Christians who need spiritual care. SWAPO serves its people and members with a chaplaincy. There are pastors and church workers who are responsible for this service. According to the head chaplain of SWAPO, the Rev. Erastus (Katalala) Haikali:

> The chaplain in SWAPO has therefore an enormous responsibility. Our party SWAPO gives us full co-operation and tries to make our work as easy as possible. SWAPO has proved that it is a responsible organization. Namibians need to have a responsible government like SWAPO. We should however admit that we experience difficulties like other freedom fighters "with no dwelling place" in exile.[19]

In further discussion with Rev. Haikali, he indicated that the SWAPO chaplaincy consists of eight pastors—four Lutherans, three Anglicans and one Catholic. Four of the pastors are serving the refugees in Angola; the other four are serving in Zambia. There are seventeen deacons; of these, four women and four men are working in Angola. The other five women and four men are working as deacons in Zambia. At the moment, they have only three theological students, one of whom is studying in Zimbabwe and the other two in Zambia.

In Zambia the SWAPO chaplaincy has to operate mostly from Nyango Refugees Centre. In Angola the main centers are: Sumbe, Talatando (Natalia Mavulu Centre) and Kwanza-Sul. Kwanza-Sul is further divided up into different centers served as outstations.

Besides Angola and Zambia, it is also the duty of the SWAPO chaplaincy to take care of the spiritual needs of Namibian students scattered all over Africa, especially in Zimbabwe, Botswana, Tanzania, and Cameroon. Namibians live not only in Africa but also overseas. Wherever these people are, they need both material and spiritual care.

"Archdeacon" and "Apostle to the Namibian Refugees" Haikali (as I call him), mentioned further difficulties of the SWAPO chaplaincy. We can summarize them as follows:

1. There is a shortage of pastors to be deployed at various centers.
2. There is a need of church buildings for conducting worship services and prayers.
3. There is lack of scholarships for theological students. Students are ready to study theology, but without money there is no way to send students to seminaries or church training centers.
4. People in exile have the urgent need to be back in a free Namibia. As long as oppression remains inside Namibia, it makes matters difficult for the SWAPO chaplaincy because people in exile, especially the youth, need more counseling and encouragement.
5. For every person, to be in exile is to be in an abnormal situation. With all this facing the workers of the SWAPO chaplaincy, Rev. Haikali gave thanks once again for the great assistance the chaplaincy receives from the Councils of Churches of African countries, especially those of Angola and Zambia. Other world bodies assist them, too, such as LWF, WDC, and benevolent fellow Christians all over the globe.

Among the SWAPO chaplaincy's worship materials, there is a small hymnbook which is divided into three parts: Lutheran songs, Catholic songs, and Anglican songs.[20]

In 1986 SWAPO, as a liberation movement waging a guerrilla war, achieved an historic milestone. A church building was erected in Nyango and consecrated for Word and Holy Sacraments in October. The ceremony was conducted by Bishop Hendrik Fredrik of the ELCSWA, assisted by the Anglican Rev. Erastus Haikali, together with his colleague Father Gerhard Heimerikx, a Catholic priest now serving within the SWAPO chaplaincy. The event at Nyango of a church consecration marked the beginning of future closer cooperation among the churches. Here was a church with a common aim of worship and praising God. The difference of denominations did not deter the people from believing that a Lutheran bishop was their bishop. The Anglican and Catholic pastors were their pastors.

One can only say that there is nothing human that is able to destroy the vitality of the worship of God. The Namibian history of suffering has not destroyed it. The hope of the church in Namibia lies wherever Namibians are to be found. The ministry of the church, on the other hand, is not caged. It is directed to all people of God irrespective of their political affiliation. Moreover, the church is a "thorn in the flesh" to those who love injustice and violate human rights.

The church in exile indicates how SWAPO is "godless" or "godly." It shows whether SWAPO is aiming to destroy the church or not. Whatever conclusions people give, the words of Dr. Alberts Maasdorp are still valid at this point, until they are proven otherwise. He said:

. . . we in the churches in Namibia have no evidence that can make us believe that SWAPO is communist or an agent of communism. We are concerned about our people who are in the movement because the majority in that movement are Lutherans, Catholics, Anglicans. . . . If SWAPO is labeled as anything it is to be labeled a national liberation movement.[21]

The Church Father Ignatius is remembered for saying that the "church is where the bishop is." One thinks of this as one remembers Bishop Colin O'Brien Winter, who was a bishop of Namibia in exile from 1972 until his death in 1981. The church in exile can well say the words of the early African theologian, Tertullian, who said that in Christian worship we believe that:

We are a body united by a common religious profession, by a godly discipline, by a bond of hope. We meet together as an assembly and congregation that as an organized force we may assail God with our prayers. Such violence is acceptable to God. We pray also for emperors [oppressors], for their ministers and those in authority, for [the people's] temporal welfare, for the peace of the world.[22]

Let people know that in worship and praying *the refugees* are compelled to refresh their memories, to stimulate their hope and to establish their confidence. At the same time they are strengthening their discipline of their sacred cause.

THE CHURCH AND PEOPLE'S RESISTANCE

Church and people's resistance is as explosive a topic as violence and non-violence. Unfortunately, those who fear resistance or vio-

lence are mostly the same people who fail to condemn institutionalized violence. "Resistance" and "violence" are traditionally defined by those who want to maintain the *status quo*. It makes it,
therefore, very hard to approach this topic objectively without
being labeled an agitator—even if one happens to resist what needs
to be resisted or is acting in self defense. In order to dilute the argument, people like to give negative parallels to the issue at stake
rather than mentioning those parallels with positive results.

In this section we shall examine visible and concrete examples of
resistance against the colonial forces imposed upon the members of
the church and society. This resistance is not something people in-
tentionally designed, but something which was forced on them.

It has already been indicated that colonialism and the colonial resistance of the Namibians came after the introduction of Christianity. Colonialism is practiced by Christians to colonize other
Christians. Resistance here is firmly rooted in the Christian faith.
We have also observed above how religion and politics in the African understanding live hand in hand. To African Christians, participation in socio–political and economic struggle is not seen as
something foreign to faith. This is part of the background of resistance.

Eight years after the German colonization of Namibia, Chief
Hendrik Wittbooi wrote a letter (dated August 4, 1892) to the English magistrate at Walvis Bay. Witbooi wanted to find out what
the true purpose of the German invasion of Namibia was. He
wrote:

I write this letter to Your Honour in the hope that you will . . .advise me of
the full truth . . . concerning the coming of the Germans; because the works
of the Germans are encroaching on my land and now even my life is threatened. They come to destroy me by war without my knowing what my guilt
is. I have been told that it is their intention to shoot me . . . perhaps you can
tell me why. . . . The German introduces laws into the land according to his
own opinion, and those laws are impossible, untenable, unbearable, unacceptable, unmerciful and unfeeling. . . . He personally punishes our people and
has already beaten people to death. . . . If possible call these people back. Because they are not following the Agreement and Resolutions on the strength
of which you let them enter this land. . . .[23]

Two years later Leutwein, the second German governor in Namibia (1894–1904), sent an ultimatum to Witbooi to recognize German supremacy. Witbooi replied that, on the one hand, he had nev-

er seen the German emperor in his life; therefore, there was no way for him to anger the emperor by words or by deeds. On the other hand, he said, God has established various kingdoms on earth. It is no sin and misdeed for him to wish to remain the independent chief of his land and people. If the Germans desired to kill him on account of his land, and without guilt on his part, that was to him "no disgrace and no damage, then I die honourably for my property." In case the Germans were going to shoot at him with their strong weapons, Witbooi had this to say:

So I will shoot back, not in my name, not in my strength, but in the name of the Lord, and under His Power. With His Help will I *defend* myself. . . . So the responsibility for the innocent blood of my people and of your people which will be shed does not rest upon me as *I have not started this war.*[24]

The answer from Leutwin was short and emphatic:

The fact that you refuse to submit yourself to the German Empire is no sin and no crime, but it is dangerous to the existence of the German Protectorate. Therefore, my dear Chief, all further letters in which you do not offer me your submission are useless.[25]

What Witbooi warned about became a reality. It is a reality felt throughout the country to this day. General von Trotha with his strong German weapons crushed the Herero at Waterberg and many fugitives fled to Botswana. The rest of the Herero were either taken prisoners of war or made slave laborers. Thousands were starved to death or executed by the Germans. Everything was done in the name of von Trotha's "Extermination Order" *(Vernichtungsbefehl)*, without exception. It reads:

Within the German boundaries, every Herero, whether found armed or unarmed, with or without cattle, will be shot—I shall not accept any more women and children. I shall drive them back to their people, otherwise I shall order shots to be fired at them. These are my words to the Herero people.

Signed: The Great General of the Mighty Kaiser, von Trotha.[26]

The Germans had a different plan for the Nama than for the surviving Herero. Hereros who survived this holocaust were to be kept as slave laborers. The fate of the Nama, to whom Wibtooi belonged as their chief, was different. Once the rebellion was over, the remaining Nama were "to be shipped to Togo or some other German colony where they will do no harm, but rather vanish from the scene in the not too distant future."[27] This idea was dropped only when the Colonial Department failed to get the necessary resources to fund the cost involved.[28] However, it was nevertheless possible to take some Namibians to these distant countries.

The final solution sought was then how to deal with the Ovambo. Their fate was to be made mine workers on a contract labor system, while the Herero were to be used on farms and the Nama were to serve as domestic servants. The whole society was thus fractured and disintegrated in many ways.

The tension between the Namibians and the European intruders continued to escalate. Between 1884 and 1907 Namibia experienced a national holocaust by the Germans. This history has never left the minds of the Namibians. Sometimes they felt it hopeless to resist, but their hope and courage to defend their rights was restored by the World Wars. The defeat of Germany in World War I strengthened the Namibians' belief that it was possible to resist the Germans successfully if they had the necessary means. Perhaps the same understanding exists among the younger generation—that it is possible to win against South Africa if they exert the necessary resistance.

The situation between the two World Wars was not a joyous one for the Namibians. Within the church, missionaries either were being pushed around, lacked funds and workers, or were cut off from the external world. Politically at this time, there was no longer any king or chief who was courageous and formidable enough to direct and uphold national aspirations. Chief Hendrik Witbooi and King Mandume gaNdemufayo were "sacrificed" for the Namibian cause. Also at this time King Nehale was dead. Chief Samuel Maherero was exiled and died in Botswana. King Iipumbu yaTshilongo was taken hostage and "imprisoned" in Okavango. In other words, both religious and political affairs were in alien hands. South Africa replaced Germany in the politics of Namibia. The transition of politics from Germany to South Africa can be looked at in relation to the people of Namibia as a fish jumping from a pan into the fire.

Those Namibians who attempted to "stick their heads above water" were mercilessly crushed, e.g., the Warmbad massacre of the Bondelswarts in 1922 and the Rehoboth mass detentions of

1924–25. King Iipumbu yaTshilongo was seized and taken hostage in 1932. These and similar suppressions made things look "quiet" because the reign of terror made itself felt throughout the country. Absence of open conflict is not equal to the absence of evil. The Namibians were stilled externally, but in their breasts burned the desire to regain their lost dignity and rights. This is a battle still in progress.

Soon after Germany gave way to South Africa, the Namibian case became the subject of international discussions, in the League of Nations and then in the United Nations. At home, Africans were being trained as teachers, pastors and evangelists for future leadership. Some of the new chiefs, like Chief Hosea Kutako, leader of the Herero Chiefs' Council, and Chief David Witbooi, son of Hendrik Witbooi "the Great," were taking up the traditional leadership of colonial resistance. The chiefs sent an Anglican priest, Michael Scott, to present the Namibian case to the United Nations in 1946. This was at the same time as the early stages of the church's emancipation from its closet of quietism.

It was at this time that a large number of Nama people left the RMS membership to join the AMEC, which they felt was the only church with open doors, willing to accommodate their human identity without color barriers. A few years later many Herero left the traditional mission of the Rhenish to form their own community (Oruuano). Seeing all this, the FMS allowed the ELCIN to be independent in 1954. Three years later the RMS found it out of fashion to keep a dependent church, partly because they had learned a lesson from secessions. By 1957 it was high time to allow the autonomy of the ELCSWA.

The spirit of Hendrik Witbooi was resurrected. Nationalism was gaining momentum. As the church became autonomous, politically there was a great urgency to have a nationalist political movement. As a result, SWANU and SWAPO were founded, of which SWAPO became the most formidable organization and a power for the colonial rule to reckon with.

Both in the church and in politics leadership was indigenized. These people were Christians. The debate was not in terms of faith; it was in terms of political and social action—whether they needed to take action or not. Compelled by their faith, most were determined to be involved in the socio–political issue of their country under colonialism and apartheid. For a while it remained to be seen what direction the church was going to take. Missionary impact was still great. While the black leadership saw that the people's resistance against social evil was part and parcel of the church's struggle for freedom and national independence, the majority of whites felt that it was heresy to mix religion and politics. This can easily be observed in a statement from Präses H. K. Diehl to the ELCSWA Synod in 1960. We take him as a representative of most missionary leadership. He said:

At the present time, politics has taken possession of the non-whites too and has stirred them up. People no longer take an interest in God's Word or His Commandments but only occupy themselves with politics; efforts are even being made to involve the church in political activity. But it is our opinion that the church must keep herself out of the political arena. . . .[29]

This quotation is indicative of the shift from missionary mentality to national aspiration by the people in Namibia. It is clear twenty years later that the shift is great. In May 1964 the two black Lutheran churches wrote a memorandum in the form of a protest against the Odendaal "homeland plan." The memorandum states:

As we consider the whole of Southern Africa to be the homeland of people of different nations and races, we believe that peace can be maintained only through close cooperation between all inhabitants of this country. We therefore ask the government to do everything in order to overcome the [prevailing] spirit of anxieties and lack of confidence and to guarantee the rights, the freedom and respect of human values.[30]

On January 23, 1967 the leaders of the Lutheran, Catholic and Anglican churches in Ovamboland wrote to the District Commander of the South African Police at Ondangwa to protest against the brutal interrogations of the people by the police, including broken bones, severe bruising, dog bites, internal damage and electric shocks.[31] Again on June 30, 1971 the two black Lutheran churches in the country addressed an open letter to then Prime Minister Mr. B. J. Vorster of South Africa to protest against apartheid and the violation of human rights and to promote the World Court's decision of bringing Namibia to independence. The letter was signed on behalf of the two church boards by Bishop Leonard Auala of the ELCIN and the Rev. Paulus Gowaseb of the ELCSWA. The Catholic and Anglican churches supported the letter.

Since the time of the open letter, the churches under the leadership of Namibians themselves have taken a clear cut stand as to what is to be done by the church in the situation of oppression and apartheid. The church made a number of representations to the government of South Africa against the violations of human rights. The Council of Churches in Namibia was created in order to speak up with one voice as a church in Namibia. The CCN represents eighty-six percent of Namibian Christians and has pleaded with the South African government and world bodies, including the United Nations, to grant Namibia independence. "As a matter of extreme urgency concerning the peace and future well-being of all people in Namibia [we appeal] that United Nations Security Council Resolution 435 is implemented without delay," said the Council of Churches in Namibia.

In the midst of resistance and institutionalized violence, according to Bishop K. Dumeni of the ELCIN, "The question today is no longer who will suffer and who will lose . . . [people] are dying daily."[33] The topic of resistance is not only history to the Namibians, it is a living reality. It is in that reality that the church has taken a stand. The church is in support of resistance against apartheid and colonialism. The church has chosen the side of the oppressed and the colonized. Church statements and press releases are crystal clear on this point, that the church in Namibia wants only one thing together with the majority of the people: that *Namibia must be free*. The church has joined the people's resistance.

THE CHURCH IN POST-INDEPENDENT NAMIBIA

Many people are asking the church in Namibia these questions: What shape will the church in Namibia take after independence? Will the church continue to be a voice of the voiceless? Will the church be ready to speak up against oppression and social injustice irrespective of who is the oppressor? Will there be any time when the church will take a neutral stand and support a *status quo?* These and similar questions are asked simply because the church in Namibia has taken the stand of siding with the oppressed. Because of the national crisis, the church in Namibia has rejected a neutral stand.

Many ask some of these questions under the impression that Namibia may be taken over by communists. Others believe that the church is against the social evil practiced in the country today simply because it is not done by blacks. That means that some ask questions determined by an ideological stand, whether the church would feel at home with capitalist or communist political leaders. This understanding is based on the prevailing belief that the church has more liberty under one form of political and economic system than the other. Those who ask these questions are more often those who live under "democratic" capitalistic administrations than those who live under "dictatorship" socialistic or communistic governments.

Bishop Dumeni of the Lutheran Church in Namibia once said, "Our problem is now." In other words, the future is not with us. What we know is the past and the present. Whatever vision people have for the future is deduced from what they know today. The church in Namibia is involved in what is necessary for people today. The future is contingent upon the present. History is made from today to the past rather than from today to the future. The future makes history when it first becomes today. What the church is doing is based on the contemporaneous and historical nature of events. To better assess the future, we have to recall past events and then analyze the present in view of the future.

It is not yet clear who will rule independent Namibia. There are many who would like to take that challenge of government, but it remains contingent upon the nature of political events. Since there is no guarantee who will rule, it is difficult to evaluate the church in post–independent Namibia.

Since the establishment of Christianity, the church has never disappeared from the globe. We may say that it has disappeared in some countries, but this we say thinking only of a church as an institution. We must be humble, because when we attempt to say that the church has disappeared we are almost saying that God has disappeared in those countries. We do see today great numbers of people coming back to the church and governments opening up doors for churches to be erected. The being of the church is God's business. It cannot be crushed by any human power. Namibians cannot preoccupy themselves with maintaining the church. They are not God. Whatever they do to keep the church functioning is just a supplement to what God is doing. It is necessary for human beings to have the church and to ask for its presence, but it is beyond their power to keep it alive. People do not protect the church, but they need its presence because it is vital to their faith.

It is in light of this background that we can talk about the church in post–independent Namibia. Namibia can be called a Christian country; the majority of its people are Christians. For more than a century these people have been oppressed by foreign governments and their surrogates. Any government which claims Namibia as free must represent the voice of the majority. The church which is part of the people will be represented among the majority of people.

The church is not based on an ideology; therefore, it cannot be equated with ideologies. The church is not even equal to democracy, but it can use democratic means to organize itself. The church in Namibia, therefore, is not scared of ideologies, but it is afraid of the misuse of ideologies — be it the misuse of capitalism or communism. A Christian can be a capitalist or a communist. Economic systems and political ideologies do not make one a Christian. These systems are usable, just like clothing. A Christian can wear a shirt made by an unbeliever, but it will not make that person an unbeliever. Any government which gives liberty to all people, including the church, and upholds justice and respects human rights, no matter what ideology it uses, will not be an enemy of the church. The church in Namibia is not struggling for a certain ideology, but it is fighting for peace, justice, equality, human dignity and human rights to prevail. For the church this is only possible when all forms of oppression, colonialism and apartheid are eradicated.

The ruling party of independent Namibia is not likely to be a new party, at least not for the next several years. One of the existing parties must rule independent Namibia. By 1975 there were about forty political parties and organizations in the country.[33] Only two of these have a more nationalist vision, namely SWANU and SWAPO, but it is SWAPO which has the higher caliber of organization and popularity both internally and internationally. It is SWAPO which is likely to rule independent Namibia. This is not to show favor to SWAPO, but rather to indicate that it is SWAPO which so far has shown the necessary qualities of mobilizing the majority. SWAPO's popularity is increasing daily, not declining. It is, therefore, possible for SWAPO to take over the administration at any time.

The church recognizes the authenticity of SWAPO. Although the church does not endorse whatever SWAPO is doing, the church is in agreement with SWAPO that Namibia must be free. The church does not agree with SWAPO for the sake of agreement, it agrees because it is a church believing in a God of justice. The church is not seeking future guarantees from SWAPO in case SWAPO takes over the government, but the church is doing what is in accordance with the gospel of love and peace. The church was never persuaded by anyone to do what it is doing now. What the church does is done under conviction of what is right to do. As a result, the church can agree with anyone who agrees on what it sees to be right and just to agree. Those who voted for Resolution 435 in the UN were not all Christians, but the church in Namibia agreed because it is a right thing to be agreed upon.

SWAPO, on its side, agrees with the church without compulsion on many issues. It is also correct to say that there are issues on which SWAPO and the church do not agree.

Besides SWAPO, there are other political parties. They may become well–organized in the future, but in my view for the time being it is necessary for them to join hands with SWAPO to bring about independence. It would be a mistake for these parties to think of SWAPO as an enemy. It would also be a mistake for SWAPO to bypass them as if they have nothing to contribute in the process of needed change.

The church in the context of change is carrying out its prophetic voice to remind all political groups and parties to unite and strive for one common goal of self–determination. In many ways the church has been disappointed by opportunistic political groups which became additional stumbling blocks in the route to freedom. However, the church has not given up. It still reminds us that the future of Namibia can be realized only if all work together as one people determined to be free.

If SWAPO is to take over, the future of the church in Namibia is clear so far. A church building among SWAPO camps is a symbol of true Christianity. A counter question can be asked if one is seeking assurance as to how far SWAPO is willing to allow the function of the church in post–independent Namibia. If SWAPO takes over, it is clear that freedom of religion and liberty of worship will prevail. It is difficult to evaluate the stand of other political parties towards the church at this moment. However, they too have never publicly indicated any intent to get rid of freedom of religion. Their parrot cry to the church with few exceptions is not to mix religion and politics.

Before we go on to other points, it is important to note the recent report of the LWF about SWAPO and the church:

It was agreed that peace, justice and respect for human rights are objectives shared by the [Namibian] churches, LWF and SWAPO. In interpreting the situation of those in exile, the LWF indicated it stands ready to visit camps of Namibian exiles and refugees. An invitation came from the president of SWAPO to do so.[34]

In post–independent Namibia the church has other concerns. Today Namibians are poor. Their poverty caused the church to be financially weak and depend heavily on support from sister churches abroad. Independence does not mean a paradise. The early years after independence will be years of hardship and reconstructing the society. This will be a painful process for the church because it will have to find ways and means to maintain itself as an institution. In view of this coming shift, it is necessary that long-range and short-term planning be done now. In the future it will also be necessary for the church to be truly independent and self-supporting. Financial planning needs to be done now so that the church can be ready for the early years of national self-determination. A church in Africa cannot be a carbon copy of a church in Europe. It may be necessary to revise the structures and administrative systems used in the churches in Namibia today.

It is important for the church to be constant and faithful. Word and sacrament will continue to be integral parts of the mission. And so long as other matters are not a matter of death and life it is possible for the church to take a neutral stance or to delay a decision. We hope the church in Namibia will be wise enough to assess these things rightly. But in the face of injustice a neutral stance will always be evil. The hope is that the church in Namibia will in all situations continue to be a voice on behalf of the voiceless and the oppressed.

NOTES

1. Claude S. Phillips, *The African Political Dictionary* (California: ABC-CLIO Information Service, 1984), 28.
2. Ibid., 81.
3. Ibid.

4. Bonifatius Haushiku, Bishop of the Roman Catholic Church in Namibia, sermon delivered at the /Ai-//Gams Ecumenical Service, Katutura, Namibia on August 31, 1986.

5. Daniel Arap Moi, President of Kenya, "Inject Church with African Culture," speech delivered at graduation ceremony at St. Paul's Theological College at Lumuru, Kenya on December 18, 1985. In *Lutheran World Information* (Geneva: LWF, 51/85), 14.

6. J. J. Kritzinger, "Sending en Kerk in Suidwes-Africa" (Pretoria), 152–61.

7. Ibid., 157.

8. Ibid., 179–83. See also Sebulon Ekandjo, "Uukamwe waVELKSWA" in *Omukwetu* (Oniipa, July 30, 1986), 6–7.

9. Shivute Usko Shivute, "20th Century Namibia" (M.A. thesis, University of Minnesota, 1985), 128.

10. Randolph Vigne, *A Dwelling Place of our Own* (London: IDAF, 1973), 11.

11. H. Bley, *South West Africa under German Rule,* trans. G. H. Ridley (London, 1971), p. 127, cited in Robin Hallett, *Africa Since 1875: A Modern History* (The University of Michigan Press, 1974), 623.

12. Kaire Mbuende, *Namibia, the Broken Shield* (Lund, 1986), 152.

13. *SWAPO Constitution,* p. 3.

14. *The Combatant* (the monthly organ of the People's Liberation Army of Namibia (PLAN) 7 (Luanda, August 1985), 7–8.

15. Ibid., 9.

16. *Namibia: A Unique Responsibility,* Highlights of United Nations action in support of Freedom and Independence for Namibia (UN Dept. of Public Information — DPI/631, undated), p. 15. See also *Namibia: The Facts* (London: IDAF, 1981), 45.

17. Alfred Babing and Hans-Dieter Brauer, *Namibia* (Dresden, 1981), 350.

18. *The Missionary Review of the World* (New York, 1921), 488; also "Rhenish Society Report" (1920/21).

19. Erastus Haikali, speech at UN Information Center. Seminar, Lusaka, Zambia on July 3, 1986.

20. Interview with Erastus Haikali (Katalala), Minneapolis, March 25, 1987.

21. *Dateline: Namibia* (New York: Division for Mission in North America, LCA, No. 3/1982).

22. Henry Bettenson. *Early Christian Fathers* (New York: Oxford University Press), 156, 141.

23. Michael Scott, *A Time to Speak* (New York, 1958), 322–23.

24. Ibid., 323.

25. Ibid., 324.

26. Vigne, p. 12. For a larger text, see Frank Parker, *South Africa: The Lost Opportunities* (Toronto: Lexington Books, 1983), 89.

27. Horst Drechsler, *Let us Die Fighting* (Berlin, 1980), 210.

28. Ibid., 211.

29. Präses H. K. Diehl, cited in Carl-J. Hellberg, *A Voice of the Voiceless* (Lund, 1979), 50.

30. Ibid., 74. See also LWF Archives-G. S. III.1.III, LWF, Correspondence, National Committee, Southern Africa, 1964—via UEM (VEM) in Wuppertal, Barmen.

31. H. Hunke and Justin Ellis, *Torture: A Cancer in our Society* (London: Catholic Institute for International Relations, 1978), 13.

32. *Omukwetu* (October 15, 1985).

33. Jorgen Lissner, ed., *Namibia 1975: Hope, Fear and Ambiguity* (Geneva: LWF, 1976).

34. *Lutheran World Information* 7/87 (Geneva: LWF, February 19, 1987), 4.